Jesus Christ

His Life and Mine

Jesus Christ

His Life and Mine

The Story of Jesus and How It Applies to Us in the *Twitter Era*

R. CHRISTIAN BOHLEN

Carpenter's Son Publishing
Franklin, Tennessee

Jesus Christ, His Life and Mine

Published by Carpenter's Son Publishing, Franklin, Tennessee. Published in association with Larry Carpenter of Christian Book Services, LLC. www.christianbookservices.com

Edited by Adept Content Solutions

Cover Design by Suzanne Lawing

Interior Layout Design by Adept Content Solutions

Printed in the United States of America

978-1-949572-00-1

To my mother, Hendrika, whose pure and constant example of faith, obedience, and love has blessed me all my days.

To my sweetheart, Helen, whose love and laughter rescued me.

To my Dutch friend, Antoon, whose faith in me and the importance of this book was unending.

Contents

Acknowledgments

Glory to the loving God of all creation, who planted and pruned me to testify of His reality and nature.

I gratefully acknowledge the heaven-sent souls who ignited my faith and guided me professionally during the production of this book—twenty years in the making.

My first realization that I was fundamentally missing something in my life occurred when I was ministering in the home of a family. My companion, Pat, who was visiting that family with me, at one point tenderly said, "*I love Jesus*." I had heard those words before, but his heartfelt testimony triggered an awareness deep in my heart that he had a true, personal knowledge of Jesus that I did not possess. I never forgot that moment. Thank you, Pat, for being an example of what childlike love for the Lord Jesus Christ looks like. By watching you, I sat up and took notice of this most central spiritual gift.

My wholehearted professional thanks go to Angela Eschler for her boundless patience and her accomplished team of editors, Michele Preisendorf, Emily Halverson, and Sabine Berlin. "Get yourself a good editor," someone once told me. Well, it took the whole village in my case! How you all labored with me and prayed over the success of this project. Your care went far beyond the professional requirement.

I also deeply appreciate the support and professionalism of all the good folks at Carpenter's Son Publishing for their veteran guidance and services. My gratitude especially to Larry Carpenter, whose faith in this project and expert care has been such a comfort, and to Lori Martinsek and Suzanne Lawing for making this a truly polished offering to God.

And if you, dear reader, were one of the nearly one hundred test readers of the early versions of this book, know that your feedback and inspiration are woven in. You shaped this book into what you are holding today. Your praise was God's voice of encouragement to say, "This is worth it; keep going."

To the real and living God who gives liberally to all who ask, I give my feeble thanks.

I love Jesus too!

A Shared Faith Perspective

As children of the same God, we share far more in common than we differ. My intent has been to ensure that this book is uplifting and doctrinally suitable for most Christian and curious non-Christian readers. During the development of this book, ministers and readers belonging to multiple Christian denominations contributed their feedback and guidance, resulting in this "shared faith perspective." It does not promote any one denominational view. Nor does it assume any prior knowledge of Jesus Christ or the Bible.

However, because there are differing views about some teachings and doctrines of Christ, readers may find it helpful to note which major positions this book takes. This book teaches that Jesus Christ is the Lord God Almighty, Creator of the heavens and earth, yet He walked the roads of ancient Israel as a man in the flesh. It teaches that believing in Him is essential, and that true faith includes worshipping Him as God and obeying Him as Master. It teaches that Jesus's ancient words are as relevant and important today as they were back then. It teaches that man is fallen and utterly unable to save himself and that the power of Christ's Atonement is what changes hearts and presents us clean before God at the last day.

This book does not teach that believing in Jesus is a one-time event, a saving moment, and that striving to live a new, holier lifestyle by following Jesus's example throughout our lives is optional. It does not teach that Jesus didn't really mean what He said or that man may dilute or diminish His teachings to suit a changing world with shifting values. As the unchangeable God, Jesus is the gold standard by which we can know what is good, what is wise, and what is truly important.

After studying and prayerfully meditating on the life and teachings of Jesus, each reader must choose his or her own church affiliation and regularly gather with the body of Christ to love, serve, and teach one another. May the Father of us all lead us in that path which He has designed for our happiness with Him in eternity.

Introduction

Regardless of why you picked up this book, you've got a hundred other things you could be doing. Whether you're a lifelong Christian or dipping your toes in the water for the first time, you're probably trying to decide whether reading this book might offer you a genuine, personalized payoff. Otherwise, why bother?

But what kind of payoff?

How about learning some facts about Christ? Hmm … In itself, that's not very rewarding.

How about a deep, personal comprehension that Jesus Christ really is the Son of God? Well, that's substantially more valuable. But we can do better than that.

How about a truly joyous life? Your life. I mean a "can't deny it, wow I love it" enthusiasm for the things of God and a fresh, bright view of yourself and your life's circumstances. Seriously.

Joy, peace, power, and light are the signature blessings of the gospel of Jesus Christ. But for years, I didn't understand how to experience these blessings. What a tragedy. I soon discovered I was not alone. This book exists to make sure those blessings are not missed. And if you already feel joy in Christ today, I testify that it can and will be deepened as you once again immerse yourself in the Master's life and teachings.

How This Book Helps

Gaining spiritual light and joy is rarely a switch-flipping, light-up moment. It's more often a gradual process, like climbing up from darkness to a well-lit place. In fact, it's a lot like working our way to the top of a climbing wall. Let's see.

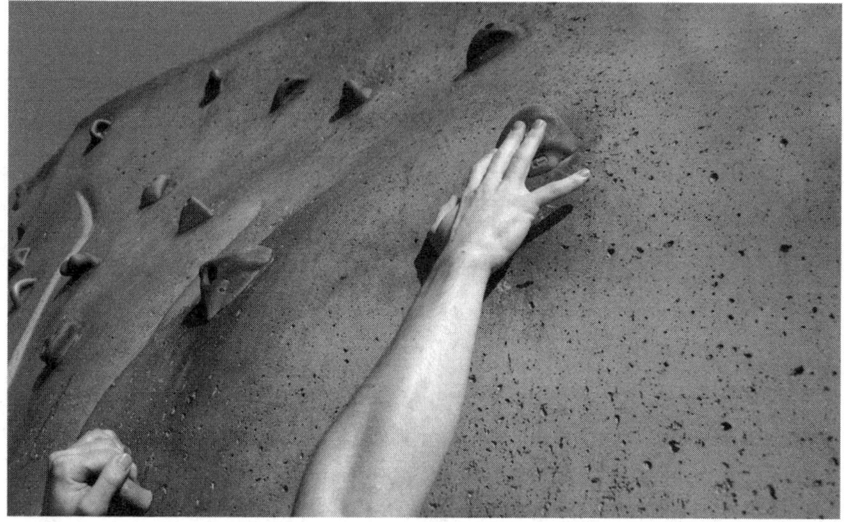

How do climbers do it? Since we humans lack the sticky fingers and toes of a tree frog, we need those odd-shaped, rubber grips and holds for our fingers, hands, and feet to help us ascend. The grips and holds are key—finger grips, hand grips, and footholds.

Too often we are trying to climb our "spiritual wall" without any grips. Or we're grasping at the wrong things. Too often we fail to realize how important it is to deeply believe in and trust the Lord Jesus Christ. And trying to believe in Jesus is really hard to do without solid spiritual grips to latch on to. As you read this book, you will encounter three types of spiritual enabling grips.

Finger grips: learn about Jesus and believe

This book walks you through the life of Christ as described in the scriptures while adding cultural and historical context. The New Testament story is brought to life with vivid imagery and a simple style that most anyone can understand. My aim is to provide just enough detail so that Jesus and His teachings come into sharp, well-lit focus.

Why is experiencing the whole birth-to-resurrection story of Jesus so important? Well, when we see His entire life unfold from beginning to end, He becomes a real person to us. We can relate to Him because of the stories, how He acted, and what He said. We can imagine how He may have felt. And we begin to feel awed.

When you see Jesus like that, and you experience the "wow, now I get it!" spiritual impressions of His true identity and greatness, it becomes far easier to believe in Him. His life and teachings form a series of grips for your fingers. Studying His life helps you see those grips. Then wrapping your "belief fingers" around each inspired impression will help you stretch higher and inch further up that wall, giving you new perspective and greater vision.

Do not underestimate the importance of intentional, focused believing in Jesus Christ and His attributes. This is a simple yet essential act that is often overlooked.

Jesus Himself taught, "Learn from me" (Matthew 11:29, NIV). This book seeks to enhance your ability to intentionally learn from Jesus—the way, the truth, and the life—and to actively, fruitfully believe in Him.

Hand grips: desire to follow Christ

Finger strength (believing in Jesus) is important, but hand strength (wanting to be like Jesus) allows us to climb higher and faster. Our genuine admiration and desire to be like Jesus helps us change in ways big and small, which begins to feel really good. We begin to feel an outside power change us, and we start to develop a new nature. We begin living on a higher plane.

We climb more fluidly, naturally, and joyously as we come to love Jesus Christ, our greatest friend and the true light of the world. His love for us becomes more real. This helps us love Him even more, which lifts us even higher. We feel more love for ourselves and then sweetly, more love for others.

Footholds: see how to follow Christ

The more real Jesus becomes to you and the nearer you feel to Him, the easier it is to follow Him. When you can see Him climbing in front of you, beckoning you upward, and when you learn to keep your eyes fixed on Him no matter what is going on around you, you'll find you can solve problems that have stumped you for years.

One of the most important goals of this book is to help you navigate whatever challenges you may be experiencing. I don't know the details of your life. But God does. At the end of nearly every chapter, I've included a brief summary of Jesus's actions, along with reflection questions, which I hope will help you relate His life and teachings to situations you might encounter in today's world. As you reflect on how the Savior faced His mission and challenges, the Spirit of God will do the rest. You will receive inspiration, ideas, and a clearer sense of what it means to follow Jesus Christ, our supreme example.

This phrase will become real, personal, and precious to you: "Come, follow me" (Matthew 4:19, NIV).

And even if you feel you are beyond the reach of hope or dead to what the power of believing in Him can do, it's okay. The teachings and life of Christ are especially for you.

The Power of Grace from the Top of the Wall

Now, let's imagine we've been given a free ride to the top of the wall. There we see Jesus, looking down and smiling compassionately on those below who believe in Him and give their best to reach higher.

We suddenly see something we hadn't noticed before. Each person who begins to believe in Jesus is instantly surrounded by a glowing, spiritual safety harness connected to Jesus ... an invisible belt that gently lifts each person higher—far beyond his or her own ability to reach, to pull up, and to push higher. This, we are told, is the grace of God that instantly takes effect when anyone believes in Jesus Christ with a sincere intention to follow Him.

Anyone who attempts to climb the wall alone cannot ever—in a million, billion years—make the climb. It is literally impossible for any man or woman.

Jesus lives in glorious light and supreme joy and wants us to enjoy it with Him. But it is only because of His grace (meaning His enabling and saving power, given to us freely) that we can and will rise to that joyous life. He wants us to climb as He climbed but He will do the heavy lifting as only He can.

The Twitter Era

Why did we draw attention to "the Twitter Era" in the subtitle of this book?

Because we all climb the walls of life within the context of our times. And we are entering an era that's dizzyingly different from anything in history. There's a phenomenon creeping in on us that's especially dangerous to our emotional, psychological, and spiritual health—a danger that's separating us from the peace, sense of self-worth, and individual guidance we could be getting from God.

Don't get me wrong. I like social media tools in small doses and for good purposes. I love all of the fingertip info and staying up on my friends' lives.

But sometimes, I don't feel better after using social media. In fact, sometimes, I feel noticeably worse.

According to the research, I'm not alone and I'm not crazy.[1]

There are a lot of warning voices emerging from credible sources backed by an increasingly thick pile of research.

Have you noticed these self-destructive tendencies creeping into your life or in others?

- Racing from one disconnected thought to another, from *app* to *post* to *tweet* to *like* to another app to *follow* to a *video* to *share*—over and over—at every free or middle-of-the-night moment
- Increasing impatience and unwillingness to focus on lengthier reading or deeper topics
- Making harsh, unkind, partially informed judgments about people or issues
- Wasting precious, God-given time by staying glued to technology
- Craving the approval of others more than the approval of God
- Being jealous of the good looks, good lives, or experiences of others
- Fear of missing out on stuff we see happening "out there"
- Worshipping our selfies and our personal preferences more than God
- … and plenty more that would be depressing to keep listing

Put this murky collection altogether, and it's leading many of us into anxiety, depression, impatience, lower self-esteem, loneliness, and a growing inability to concentrate for sustained periods—so says the research.[2]

Perhaps ugliest of all, we are increasingly disconnected from God and disconnected from each other. The illusion of connectedness and fulfillment through technology is just that. It is an illusion. We're often losing touch with ourselves and our true identity. We're at risk of being mentally shredded and sifted like wheat. (See Luke 22:31.)

Finding Peace in the Twitter Era

So, what's all this have to do with Jesus?

In every era, man's spiritual purpose has been to recognize and rise above the darkness of their times by climbing into God's eternal light. Jesus is always relevant because His way is always the way up and out of darkness, *any* kind of darkness in any era.

Jesus helps us find God, our Heavenly Father. He helps us reconnect and stay connected to our true selves—as children of God. He helps us connect with each other—as brothers and sisters. He helps us live with love—by focusing on what matters most. He helps us prioritize our time, our desires, and our actions.

Believing and following Jesus turns on a light switch in our souls that helps us recognize and choose right over wrong and wisdom over foolishness—even in our modern times. This is the key resounding message of this entire book!

Even in the Twitter era, Jesus shows the way up and out of the darkness so that we can become what we were meant to become. He restores peace, happiness, and a sense of our self-worth that's divine and untouchable compared to worldly wisdom with its fickle infatuations.

Here We Go

Your climbing wall awaits. The grips have been carefully placed on every page of this book.

Begin your climb with the Master and watch as the light of Jesus grows brighter and tastes sweeter than ever before.

In time, may your heart whisper in celebration, "It's a miracle! His life is lifting and saving mine."

Author's Note

To aid us in applying the teachings of Jesus in our lives, most chapters begin with a scripture followed by one or more by reflection questions. At the end of each chapter, you may wish to journal about the inspired, personalized impressions and motivation you experience as you read and reflect.

I testify that finding some quiet time to immerse yourself in the life of Jesus Christ and following the "climbing wall" process described in this introduction can work miracles in your life.

I have been supremely blessed during my years spent writing this book. I will never forget the uniquely happy feelings that enveloped my every thought as I prayed and I wrote. My walk with Jesus during these challenging years has changed my life and the lives of those around me. Pondering how His life relates to real-life modern situations has brought peace, insights, and positive behavioral changes into my life.

May His light fill you and every other soul within your circle of family and acquaintances.

Part One

Entering the World's Stage

Love from Above

And this is his commandment, that we should believe on the name of his Son Jesus Christ.

—1 John 3:23

My Upward Climb

Do I really believe on the name of Jesus?

Chapter 1
Before Christ

Imagine opening a set of doors at the back of your head, walking in, and finding a seat. Welcome to your inner movie theater. You know, the one that plays the best kinds of movies, the ones you never forget.

Once envisioned—no, *experienced*—the story of the life and teachings of Jesus Christ cannot be erased. It is too grand. It transcends sight, sound, and emotion. Why? Because Jesus Christ adds the dimension of eternal light. In a tender, deeply satisfying way, it blows any IMAX movie experience out of the water. It's that much better.

Grab your favorite seat in that mental movie theater of yours, keep a hand on your heart, and get ready. Even if this is a repeat performance for you, it's still the *greatest story ever told*.

Popcorn is optional.

The Setting

Let's go back to the land of Israel about two thousand years ago. The iron-fisted Romans ruled the land, and the inhabitants were sick of it, but there was little they could do.

Caesar, the Roman leader, had no tolerance for rebellion. His soldiers were brutal instruments of punishment, controlling an enormous ring of nations in every direction, including much of modern Europe, North Africa, Egypt, Syria, and more. It was not uncommon to see fields covered with hundreds, even thousands, of people being crucified—hanging on crosses in agony for days until freed by death. It was their penalty for insurgence and a grim warning to passersby.

Can you imagine such a scene?

Who, Exactly, Lived in Israel?

The Israelites got their name from Jacob, grandson of Abraham. Because of his faithfulness, the Lord changed Jacob's name to Israel, meaning "let God prevail." This blessed and favored man of God had twelve sons. Their families multiplied, and before long, there were twelve huge tribes, one named after each son. They became known as the twelve tribes of Israel. Problems arose as these tribes moved into enemy territory. Over the years, they were conquered by nation after nation and were either killed or taken captive and carried away to other lands. By the time the Romans conquered Israel, there wasn't much left of the original Israelite nation.

Ten of the tribes were largely scattered during those conquests, and to this day nobody is sure where their descendants are. The main tribe left in Israel was Judah, as well as remnants of a tribe named Benjamin. At this point in history, other nations simply referred to them as "the Jews" (meaning "of the tribe of Judah" and "dwellers in Jerusalem").

The Jews loved the stories of their history, like when God and Moses crushed the Egyptians. Despite their sufferings, they remained deeply religious. Through all their struggles, they continued to believe that God would bless them above all nations—for so it was told them by God's prophets—but only if they were good and faithful.[3]

The Romans thought the Jewish beliefs were nonsense, but they let them practice their religion as long as they didn't challenge Roman authority. To the Jews, however, having such freedoms granted wasn't the same as having their own nation, and they desperately wanted to be free.

The Messiah

Every prophet before this time had taught that an important prophet would come[4]—someone even greater than Moses. This prophet would deliver the Israelites out of bondage and become their great governor. Moses himself said that whoever would not listen to Him would be held accountable before God. (See Deuteronomy 18:15, 18–19.)

This prophet came to be known as the Messiah. Every Jew knew of these prophecies and looked forward to His coming. A problem developed, however. Over the years, the Jews' understanding of what the Messiah would be like got off track.

Although the prophets had taught that the Messiah would be the Son of God, this understanding was mostly lost. In Christ's day, the Israelites came to believe He would be a powerful, mortal king—like a superior version of Moses—who would demolish their enemies in battle and lead the people of Israel to their rightful place above all other nations in the world, resulting in an earthly paradise.[5]

How It Applies to Me

I Got Cheated, or Did I?

Consider for a minute: what if you expected to receive the latest, hottest electronic gadget or the present of your dreams for Christmas, but instead you got something your parents felt would make you "truly happy?"

Disappointed? Shocked? Maybe a "you're kidding!" reaction? In a sense, the people of Israel were expecting a fabulous gadget but got something entirely different—the teachings and glorious example of the Son of God. Although the gift was a million times more valuable than any cool and flashy gadget, they couldn't see it because they wanted and expected something else. They expected something to make their lives glorious and easier, not something to make their souls purer and more heavenly.

Recognizing the value of the gift would take a little humility and patience. It would be easy to throw it out and say, "Well, that's not what I wanted." But at what cost?

The Announcement

North of Jerusalem, in a hilly region dotted with small towns, stood an unremarkable town called Nazareth. It was a simple Jewish farming community with less than five hundred inhabitants, where many were related and likely knew each other.[6]

It was here in this ordinary place that two seemingly ordinary people, Mary and Joseph, were engaged to be married. Through them, the prophecies regarding the Messiah were about to be fulfilled.

Mary and Joseph spent their days apart from each other, which was common back then for engaged couples who had not yet consummated their marriage.

Let's go back to that ancient time and place and walk along those fertile fields past farmers bent over in their labors. We enter Nazareth and walk among clay-colored stone-and-brick structures, past women and children with water pots, and come to a private setting where we find Mary, alone in her thoughts, going about her daily chores and tending to prayers.

Watch now as if you are there. See Mary slowly lifting her eyes from her work, becoming aware of a light and another presence in the room. She gazes in growing astonishment at a bright, glorious-looking personage hovering in the air quite near her, dressed in white. Look up now—right from where you are sitting—and imagine this happening to you this very instant. The angel speaks:

> *"Hail, thou that art highly favored, the Lord is with thee: blessed art thou among women."*
>
> *And when she saw him, she was troubled at his saying …*
>
> *And the angel said unto her, "Fear not, Mary: for thou hast found favor with God." (Luke 1:28-30)*

Mary is "troubled at his saying," meaning she's feeling uncertain about what is happening and wonders what the angel means.

The angel continues:

> *"And, behold, thou shalt conceive in thy womb, and bring forth a son, and shalt call his name Jesus.*

"He shall be great, and shall be called the Son of the Highest: and the Lord God shall give unto him the throne of his father David:

"And he shall reign over the house of Jacob for ever; and of his kingdom there shall be no end." (Luke 1:31-33)

The angel's mention of "his father David" is significant. It was common knowledge among the Jews that the Messiah would be a descendant of King David, and Mary was a direct descendant of that famous king from Israel's days of glory. (See Luke 3:23–38.) But could *she* really be the mother of the Messiah? The statement from the angel could not be understood otherwise.

She then asks the angel a question.

"How shall this be, seeing I know not a man?" (Luke 1:34)

Mary is asking how she could possibly give birth—as an unmarried virgin—because she has not "known" a man.

And the angel answered and said unto her:

"The Holy Ghost shall come upon thee, and the power of the Highest shall overshadow thee: therefore also that holy thing which shall be born of thee shall be called the Son of God ... For with God nothing shall be impossible." (Luke 1:35, 37)

Every part of this must be amazing to Mary. Not only will she have a child prior to consummating her marriage, but He will be the Son of God. Again, that's the *Son* of *God*. We hear that phrase so often we may lose the enormity of what it really means. But this is not going to be an everyday child. This is monumental.

Mary, an ordinary woman from a small, ordinary town, is told she will give birth to the Messiah, the literal Son of God, the Father of all. Mary bravely and tenderly answers:

"Behold the handmaid of the Lord; be it unto me according to thy word. And the angel departed from her." (Luke 1:38)

Mary's answer is the perfect expression of respect and humility, saying, in effect, "Here I am, the willing servant of God. I accept this responsibility and believe it will happen as you have told me."

Joseph's Discovery

For some reason, even though Joseph and Mary were engaged to be married, God did not inform Joseph of what was happening. And it appears Mary did not tell Joseph either. Perhaps the angel directed her not to tell anyone and that was not recorded in our scriptures. We just don't know.

Sometime after becoming pregnant, Mary went to visit her cousin Elizabeth, who lived some distance away. When she returned to Nazareth about three months later, the infant Son of God was alive and growing inside Mary's womb. No doubt her belly had swollen so that when she returned, Joseph realized that she was with child.

We don't know what conversations they may have had. The scriptures make it clear, however, that Joseph struggled in knowing how to deal with this. He was very close to ending their engagement, planning to do it as privately as possible—which would have been to his disadvantage but possibly saved Mary from stoning. To end their engagement without publicly blaming Mary would have required Joseph to give the dowry and "bride price" money to Mary and her family anyway, assuming the Nazarenes followed the Jewish customs of the day.[7] No wonder the scriptures refer to Joseph as a righteous man. (See Matthew 1:19.) Even in this distressing situation, Joseph thought first about Mary's well-being. But then we read:

> *While he thought on these things, behold, the angel of the Lord appeared unto him in a dream, saying, "Joseph, thou son of David, fear not to take unto thee Mary thy wife: for that which is conceived in her is of the Holy Ghost.*
>
> *"And she shall bring forth a son, and thou shalt call his name Jesus: for he shall save his people from their sins." (Matthew 1:20-21)*

Whereas Mary's visit from the angel was an actual, in-person visit—possibly in the light of day—Joseph received his message in a dream. No matter, they both knew God had reached out to them personally and wanted them to understand and embrace this important and most unusual responsibility.

How It Applies to Me

Courage One Day at a Time

Did you get a roadmap when you were born showing you exactly what to do with your life? I'm guessing not.

On any given day, anything can happen. We just don't know what's around the next corner. It's a little unsettling sometimes.

We may not know, but God certainly does. Notice how the angel told Joseph, "Fear not to take unto thee Mary thy wife." God knew how Joseph felt; He knew of Joseph's understandable concern and helped him through it. It is often said that "God knows the end from the beginning."

What did Mary and Joseph actually know about what lay before them? What would it mean to have the Son of God born to them? Would life be easier because of this privilege or more challenging?

Mary and Joseph had to navigate life a day at a time, just like all of us.

Love from Above

Believe ***on*** *the name of Jesus,*
Believe ***in*** *the name of Jesus,*
Believe on the name of His Son, Jesus Christ.

—New Testament (bold added)

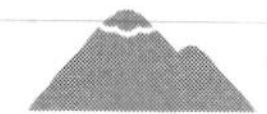

My Upward Climb

How important is the act of believing in Christ to me?

Is that a box I mentally checked years ago,
thinking that was all there was to it?

Do I know what it really means to "believe on the name of Jesus?"

Chapter 2

The Lamb of God

Sometime after the angel's announcement to Mary, the spirit of the soon-to-be-born Son of God left the presence of the Father and entered into a tiny, growing form within His earthly mother's womb.

Do you think our heavenly Father will be careless about the earthly conditions into which He sends His Son? Or will He carefully choose those conditions to teach us about His ways and His character? Will the very manner of Christ's birth help us understand Him and believe in Him?

The Road to Bethlehem

Many years before Joseph and Mary lived in Nazareth, the prophet Micah wrote:

> *But thou, Beth-lehem ... though thou be little among the thousands of Judah, yet out of thee shall he come forth unto me*

> *that is to be* ***ruler in Israel****; whose goings forth have been from of old, from everlasting. (Micah 5:2, bold added)*

This "ruler in Israel" was understood by the Jews to be the Messiah. This prophecy from Micah made it clear that the Messiah would be born in Bethlehem, also known as the city of David.

But Joseph and Mary lived in Nazareth, about eighty miles away from Bethlehem. How could the Savior's birth fulfill this prophecy?

While Joseph and Mary were engaged, an order had come from the government in Rome: everyone in Israel was required to travel to the city of their ancestors to be counted for a census. Both Joseph and Mary were descendants of David, so to Bethlehem they would go, even though Mary was near to delivery.

What must she have been feeling as they prepared for the journey? What if she had the baby during the trip? Along the road? Nevertheless, the law was the law, and to the census they went, eighty miles, on foot, requiring at least five *days* of walking.

The people of that time were used to walking long distances, but a pregnant Mary? It had to be a great trial. Instead of a luxurious carriage, Joseph tenderly helped her onto the back of a donkey. How must Mary have felt, bouncing and wobbling while trying to protect the holy life in her womb for eighty dusty miles? Even though Mary would soon give birth to the Creator Himself, she had to endure these pains and challenges, just like any other woman.

As they neared the bustling town of Bethlehem, they sought a place of rest, a place of comfort. But the little place was full of census goers, and room for sleeping was scarce. Just in time, they found a place to stay, but very likely it was not what they imagined.

Jesus, the Messiah, was born into a tiny, earthly body.

Making Sense of Scripture

No Room in the Inn

You've probably seen versions of the Christmas story where irritated innkeepers turn Mary away, even in her condition, saying, "No room in the inn!" It turns out that it probably didn't happen that way.

The word in the Bible we see translated as "inn" most likely referred to a sleeping compartment in what was known as a "khan." Khans were places where travelers could stay with their animals. Instead of having closed rooms, as we would expect in a hotel today, a khan had open sleeping compartments surrounding an inner court where the travelers' animals were kept. Mary and Joseph may have been unable to find space in one of the compartments, so they may have spent the night in the central area near their animals.[8]

There are other places Jesus may have been born. Early Christian traditions suggest that Jesus was born in a cave just outside Bethlehem. For years, caves had been used by shepherds and other travelers and their animals, so it's not surprising they would find a manger inside such a cave.[9]

The Lowly Shepherds

Not far from Mary, Joseph, and the baby Jesus, the hills surrounding Bethlehem were dotted with shepherds and their sheep, tucked in for a sleep.

Even though Abraham, King David, and other respected Israelite leaders had been shepherds, in Jesus's day, shepherds were not respected. You didn't want your daughter or son to grow up and marry a shepherd. For many reasons we would now consider silly and unfair, they were considered untrustworthy and unclean.[10] But that's not how God saw them. For a few of Bethlehem's shepherds, this night would be unforgettable.

Imagine now the quiet of the night that the shepherds enjoy. Hour after hour, crickets chirp as sheep huddle together in rest, uttering an occasional bleat. Then suddenly the sky brightens supernaturally, the light surrounding them, and an angel dressed in white appears out of nowhere, hovering above them in the air:

> *The angel of the Lord came upon them, and the glory of the Lord shone round about them: and they were sore afraid. And the angel said unto them, "Fear not: for, behold, I bring you good tidings of great joy, which shall be to all people." (Luke 2:9-10)*

No wonder they are "sore afraid," probably faltering backward as their flailing arms shield their faces against the brightness. The angel continues:

> *"For unto you is born this day in the city of David [which is Bethlehem] a Saviour, which is Christ the Lord. And this shall be a sign unto you; Ye shall find the babe wrapped in swaddling clothes, lying in a manger."*
>
> *And suddenly there was with the angel a multitude of the heavenly host praising God. (Luke 2:11-13)*

It is incomprehensible yet beautiful. We can imagine the shock giving way to peace and reverence as the shepherds gradually calm down and glance at each other, listening, and venturing a smile. God really has sent angels to them, they realize, announcing that the Christ is born.

The Christ, born tonight? Generations have waited for this moment, and here it is, tonight? It is almost beyond belief yet undeniably real.

Following the instructions of the angel, the shepherds quickly run to nearby places in search of a manger, like the khan in the city or the caves where they often take shelter. We don't know what other instructions the angel may have given them, but somehow they find the young family. Perhaps as they reach the birthplace they recognize the sign that was given and stop to catch their breath, leaning against the walls.

Their eyes meet those of Joseph and then Mary, who look up to find the shepherds staring reverently at their new child. The place is hush-quiet, with a donkey looking placidly on, its ear twitching slightly. Perhaps other traveling companions are lying on the ground nearby. The shepherds humbly ask permission to come closer, and they see Him plainly: the promised baby, lying in a manger of all places. The sign is fulfilled, and they know for certain. *It is the Christ child.*

Perhaps after a respectful silence, one of the shepherds tells Joseph what has just happened and how they've found them. We see Joseph and Mary exchanging surprised glances and looking again at the winded shepherds, whose eyes glisten, full of the heavenly vision. The shepherds kneel near the manger as they relate what the angels told them: "In the city of David … ye shall find the babe wrapped in swaddling clothes, lying in a manger" (Luke 2:12).

Not surprisingly, the shepherds spread the news so that others would know that the Christ who would deliver Israel had been born.

> *And when they had seen it, they made known abroad the saying which was told them concerning this child. (Luke 2:17)*

Making Sense of Scripture

The Names and Titles of Jesus[11]

Names in the scriptures often have rich meaning. Given the importance of the phrase "Believe on the name of Jesus," let's carefully consider just five out of the dozens of the names and titles used to describe Jesus in scripture.

Jesus. The Hebrew name "Yeshua" (translated today as "Jesus") was very common at the time of His birth. In America, it would be as common as John or Mike. But the root meaning of the name is "to rescue" or "to save." Recall that an angel specifically told Joseph what to name his newborn step-Son, clearly referencing this important meaning of His name: "Thou shalt call his name JESUS: for he shall save his people from their sins" (Matthew 1:21).

Christ. You may think that "Christ" is simply Jesus's last name, like Smith or Williams. Not so. More correctly, Jesus is referred to in scripture and other historical records as "Jesus, *the* Christ."

"Christ" is not really a name; it's a title that means "the anointed one." In ancient times, a prophet or another person with authority would place oil on the head of the new king as a symbol of his being chosen to fulfill this role. The title "Christ" meant that Jesus was the anointed King of all, chosen by the Father to save the entire family of God's children from spiritual and physical death. And, ultimately, He would physically rule over all the earth. The title "Christ" is an extremely important and holy word.

Messiah. The title "Christ" is a Greek translation of the Hebrew word *Messiah*. The words *Christ* and *Messiah* mean precisely the same thing. (Hebrew is the original language of the Jews.)

Son of God. As one of the three members of the Godhead, Jesus is fully God yet also the Son of God the Father.[12] Jesus is also referred to as the only begotten of God. (*Begotten* means "physically born." Read Luke 1:31–35 for an additional description of this.) The Holy Ghost or Holy Spirit is the third member of the Godhead.

Lamb of God. In the Old Testament, the Israelites were commanded to offer the best of their lambs to God—only those without defect. This sacrificing of sheep was a symbol, a foreshadowing, of the great sacrifice of Jesus, often called the Lamb of God, who was also without any defect.

Power in the Sacred Name of Jesus Christ

The frequent commandment to "believe on His name" must be very important, considering how often that phrase and similar ones are used throughout the scriptures. I testify that simply believing on His *name* begins to fill us with light and power to change—whether we feel like we know Him yet or not. It is a place to start. It activates a switch that begins the flow of light. When we quietly and intentionally flex our belief muscle by thinking, "I believe in Jesus Christ. I believe in Jesus Christ …," we take the first steps toward our heavenly home.

Believing *on* His name also suggests to our minds that we are building on a sure foundation, that we rest on something secure—like the Rock of Ages, as Jesus is often called. Meditating on His many holy names and their rich meanings can fill us with beautiful, worshipful feelings. (See also Faith in the Lord Jesus Christ, p. 60)

The Exemplary Birth of Jesus Christ

It seems appropriate that Jesus was born in a place among shepherds. Lambs are not aggressive; they are meek and peaceful. They follow and obey just like Jesus, whose perfect obedience to the Father enabled Him to become our example and our savior. Soon, He would become the Good Shepherd to the entire human family.

His Life and Mine

What Did Jesus Do?

- Jesus left a perfect, heavenly life to live with us and teach us in person, despite the pains and discomforts He knew He would face.
- Jesus didn't make a grand entrance to prove by His power and magnificence that He was God. His birth was announced to a lowly and humble people—not to the kings of the earth, but to a small group of shepherds.
- Jesus's first act on earth—His birth—was the embodiment of humility.

What Would I Do?

- Like Jesus, am I willing to sacrifice things that are important to me for the good of my family and friends? When I think of what Jesus gave up, does that make my sacrifices seem a little easier?
- Does humility come naturally to me? Or does that word make me cringe just a little? Should it become a higher priority?
- When I see people online saying brash and arrogant things, am I careful not feed into that or allow those voices to lead me away from the simple, quiet wisdom of God?
- Do I take time during my prayers and quiet time to say, "Heavenly Father, I believe in Jesus Christ whom you have sent. I believe in Jesus Christ"? Do I say it frequently in my mind? Do I regularly say it, exercise it, mean it, and allow that conviction to fill me?

Love from Above

"For God so loved the world, that he gave his only begotten Son, that whosoever believeth in him should not perish, but have everlasting life."

—John 3:16

My Upward Climb

Have I sincerely thanked Heavenly Father for sending His Son, Jesus Christ, so that I might have everlasting life?

Have I asked the Father to help me understand all that I am studying about Jesus?

Chapter 3

Wild Man Preaching

Though we know very little about Jesus's early years, we do know that He was part of a rather large family. He was the oldest of five sons, and He had at least two sisters (see Mark 6:3). Joseph, His stepfather, was a craftsman of some kind, likely a carpenter, and Jesus followed in his footsteps. They served the people of His hometown of Nazareth by constructing various useful or beautiful things.

Perhaps most importantly, we know that Jesus was spiritually perfect. He was one hundred percent free of sinful thought or behavior (see Hebrews 4:15). We can be certain that even as a boy and young man, Jesus was perfectly honest, obedient to God's commandments, kind toward others, respectful toward his parents, and chaste in his thoughts, and He displayed every other virtuous attribute we can think of. How otherwise can one be free of sin?

We also have this one, brief scripture that tells us a great deal:

> *And Jesus increased in wisdom and stature, and in favor with God and man. (Luke 2:52, NKJV)*

How interesting that He "increased in favor with man." Before acting in His role as the Messiah, it appears that His neighbors in Nazareth liked and respected Him as a very good boy and an upright young man.

Growing Up in Nazareth

For some reason, Nazareth was not a town the people of Jesus's day respected. In fact, the whole region of Galilee, which included Nazareth, was considered inferior, possibly because of its history of Gentile populations that often surrounded the area and at times squeezed the Israelites out.[13] Why else did people sometimes struggle to take Jesus seriously, saying things like, "Can any good thing come out of Nazareth?" or throw out insults like, "Art thou also of Galilee?" (See John 1:46 and John 7:52.)

However, growing up in Nazareth may have had its advantages. The town overlooked an important international road through the Jezreel Valley. There would have been a steady stream of people with interesting stories, caravans full of goods, and news from other countries. You can think of it as an interstate highway through the old world. Nazareth was also next to one of Galilee's capital cities, Sepphoris, just four miles away, with a population of about thirty thousand encompassing a significant Roman presence, politicians, social elites, and traders who engaged in diverse languages.

It's very possible that the townspeople, including Jesus, were able to stay in touch with the politics and trends of the day because they were so close to this flow of foreigners and news. This could have been important to Jesus as He learned about the outside world and prepared for His great mission.[14]

Crying in the Wilderness

When Jesus was about thirty years old, a strange thing happened. The scriptures tell of a man who was heard "crying in the wilderness" (see John 1:23), not weeping, but crying, in the Old English sense of the word: "to announce with a loud voice." This man wasn't teaching in the temple or cities. Huge crowds went out of their way to go where he was preaching in the wilderness by the banks of the river Jordan.

For hundreds of years before the birth of Jesus, there hadn't been prophets in Israel—not one single prophet that we know of—and the Jews had gotten used to it being that way. They knew the stories about past prophets, like Moses and Isaiah, and probably imagined what a prophet might look like in their day, but no one at that time would have really expected to see or hear a prophet. Yet here he was, "crying in the wilderness."

The Jews became extremely curious. This man wore crude clothing and looked like he came straight out of the desert. In fact, he did come out of the desert. The prophets of years past were sometimes the same—living in wild places and wearing rough clothing. So when people saw him preaching, they probably thought, "Well, he *looks* like he could be a prophet."

He gained so much attention that the leaders of the Jews sent messengers to ask him who he was:

> *Then they said to him, "Who are you, so that we may give an answer to those who sent us? What do you say about yourself?"*
>
> *He said, "I am A VOICE OF ONE CRYING IN THE WILDERNESS, 'MAKE STRAIGHT THE WAY OF THE LORD,' as Isaiah the prophet said." (John 1:22-23, NASB)*

This was a stunning answer.

The man was John the Baptist. The prophet Isaiah had foretold John's important role as the prophet "crying in the wilderness" and saying, "Prepare ye the way of the Lord" (Isaiah 40:3). John plainly told them that he was that voice and that he was fulfilling Isaiah's prophecy, preparing the way for the Messiah.

To the leaders of the Jews, this was a grand and lofty claim, which they viewed with great skepticism.

Doctrinal Points to Ponder

God the Merciful

God knew that the teachings of Jesus would be very different from what the people had learned from their leaders. He knew it would be difficult for many to believe and understand His Son.

Because John the Baptist acted and looked like the prophets of old, it was easier for the people to believe him. He helped them transition from the old ways to the new. His testimony was powerful, in-your-face evidence that they'd better listen to the man coming after him—the very Messiah.

The fact that God sent John the Baptist to prepare the way shows that God is merciful and reasonable. He will never force truth on us, yet He always provides witnesses and evidence to help us find truth and believe.

John the Bold

"Repent, for the kingdom of heaven is at hand!" John cried (Matthew 3:2, NKJV). He baptized all who were willing to listen and change their lives—and there were many. He declared:

> *"As for me, I baptize you with water for repentance, but He who is coming after me is mightier than I, and I am not fit to remove His sandals; He will baptize you with the Holy Spirit and fire." (Matthew 3:11, NASB)*

No one had heard powerful, bold teachings like John's in years, nor was it common to speak out against the leaders of the Jews like John did. He called them a "generation of vipers" and warned them of the consequences of not repenting (see Luke 3:7).

The common people generally accepted John as a prophet, but John's message angered the leaders. They didn't like being pushed to the side, and most of the leaders refused to believe him.

Making Sense of Scripture

Why Repentance?

Why did John tell the people they needed to repent? What were they doing that was so bad?

First of all, everyone needs repentance—not just "bad" people.

Since about four hundred years before the coming of Christ, the scribes and rabbis had been the teachers in Israel. They were well educated in the scriptures. Some of these teachers belonged to a group called the Pharisees, who believed they were better than everyone else because of all the little rules they kept (like not being allowed to walk more than a certain number of steps on the Sabbath day). There were literally hundreds of these rules.

Because of these fanatical and misguided teachers, many Jews lost sight of the true purpose of their faith. They were careful about meaningless things, but they sinned in big ways. So John told them they needed repentance.

To repent means to "stop going the wrong direction, turn around, and don't go back to your old ways." John gave many examples of what to do and not do, as prophets always do. (See Luke 3:7–20.)

John was preparing the people to understand and accept Jesus. If our lives are filled with selfish, dishonest, or unclean thoughts and actions, it's like trying to see through a filthy window: we won't be able to recognize the truth. John was sent to wash the people's hearts and minds so they could recognize, understand, and accept the Son of God. That's how he prepared the way.

The Baptism of Jesus

Let's stand near the banks of the river and watch, looking down at John the Baptist, waist-deep in the water, crying out and gesturing to the crowds around him to come and be baptized.

A long line of people inch their way toward him, like camels approaching an oasis after a long desert trek. He lowers each one into the river, and then they come out, filled with joy and embracing their family and friends. The scene is peaceful and reverent. The place seems holy.

Then, a man—unknown to the crowd—walks into the water toward John, and they stop to speak. John pauses, and then we hear John ask the man:

> *"I have need to be baptized by You, and do You come to me?"*
>
> *But Jesus answering said to him, "Permit it at this time; for in this way it is fitting for us to fulfill all righteousness." Then he permitted Him. (Matthew 3:14-15, NASB)*

In that moment, as you hear those words, do you have any doubt that John knows that the man standing in front of him is superior to him? Can he tell that the man, Jesus, is completely free from sin? Nevertheless, at Jesus's urging, John baptizes him.

> *And Jesus, when he was baptized, went up straightway out of the water: and, lo, the heavens were opened unto him, and he saw the Spirit of God descending like a dove, and lighting upon him: and lo a voice from heaven, saying, "This is my beloved Son, in whom I am well pleased." (Matthew 3:16-17)*

Close your eyes and hear the Father's voice as it would have been—caring, dignified, and reverent. Can you feel the love He has for His Son? Can you feel the peace He is bestowing upon the world? At this moment, John knows beyond doubt that this is the Christ for whom he has prepared the way. (Although Jesus and John were second cousins, it's not clear whether they spent any time together before this moment. See Luke 1 for a fascinating story about their mothers meeting when both were pregnant.)

Doctrinal Points to Ponder

Jesus the Obedient

Even though He was sinless, Jesus persuaded John to baptize Him so He could show us that baptism is essential for everyone. Jesus is our example in every aspect of life, and that included being obedient to the Father and being baptized.

John the Faithful Witness

Sometime after baptizing Jesus, John announced to his followers, "His voice gives me happiness; my joy is fulfilled in seeing His success. He stands at the beginning of His ministry; I am near the end of mine. He must increase but I must decrease. He came from heaven and therefore is superior to all things of earth; the Father loves Him and has given all things into His hands" (John 3:28–36, condensed and paraphrased).

This great and humble man, John the Baptist, prepared the people of Israel by cleansing their hearts and repeatedly testifying that Jesus was the actual Messiah. Then he willingly stepped into the background.

His Life and Mine

What did Jesus do?

- As child, young man, and throughout His life, Jesus was morally clean and a person of complete integrity. In every thought and action, He showed respect, love, and honor to God, His parents, and villagers. He was continually positive, kind, and compassionate and didn't engage in idle or negative talk about others. How do we know? Because these are the attributes of one who is "without sin."
- Jesus understood that evidence and witnesses are appropriate and necessary in supporting our ability to believe in Him. (See 2 Corinthians 13:1.)
- Jesus showed us by His example that it is important to be obedient to God and be baptized by one having authority.

What would I do?

- What if I have a few favorite sins that I simply don't want to change or don't believe I can change? Does Jesus's example of godly living help me to humble myself and deepen my righteous desires? Do I believe it or do I dismiss it?
- Do I know the difference between seeking a sign to prove spiritual truths and recognizing God-given evidence and witnesses and then choosing to believe?
- If I'm weighing whether to be baptized or not, does Jesus's example in being baptized make the decision clearer?
- Who do I know that may benefit from a discussion about spiritual evidence or why it is important to obey God?
- When I interact on social media, can I imagine Jesus as a young man, living today, with a smartphone in hand? He lived wisely in His day. Can His example help me live wisely today?

Love from Above

We have a great high priest, that is passed into the heavens, Jesus the Son of God … [who] was in all points tempted like as we are, yet without sin.

—Hebrews 4:14–15

My Upward Climb

Do I comprehend and believe that Jesus was sinless and truly my perfect example?

Can I picture Him above me, smiling and waving me higher?

Chapter 4

Temptations

Jesus was about thirty years old when He was baptized. Immediately after, He recognized it was time for Him to leave Nazareth, begin actively teaching, and do what He was sent to do. Thus far, He had enjoyed a normal small-town life. Suddenly, everything would change.

Jesus apparently waited until he was thirty years old because that was the age when Jewish priests were permitted to begin their service.[15] Preaching at a younger age would likely have been considered inappropriate—and one more reason for enemies to accuse Him. Regardless of why, this was His time, and He needed power and direction from the Father who sent Him.

No person on earth could prepare the Son of God for His mission. He went to the one place where He could receive private instruction—the wilderness. In Jesus's time, people referred to any place without inhabitants as a "wilderness."[16] It could have been a vast plain, a mountain, or a desert region. We don't know. He probably packed light for the trip—with no food at all—because He chose to fast for forty days.

How It Applies to Me

Why Fasting?

When people fast, they eat no food for one or more days. A practical way to get started with fasting is to skip two meals for approximately twenty-four hours. But does it really do any good?

Yes, actually, it does a lot of good. When we fast, we strive to pay no attention to the needs or wants of the body. We don't have to think about preparing meals (and we try not to think about being hungry).

I have found that my spirit is much more open to inspiration when I fast. My mind is clearer too. I receive and recognize answers to questions more easily. Fasting is an excellent thing to do before making important decisions. It helps us keep our highest priorities—the things of eternity—first in our lives.

The Tempter

Although Jesus went to the wilderness to be with His Father and nobody else, He encountered an uninvited guest. We are all visited by this guest from time to time. He is a troublemaker, intent on doing us harm, a spoiler of good goals and righteous desires.

No person ever born was capable of doing the good that Jesus was sent to do. And nobody hates good and wants to stop it more than the Devil, also known as Satan, Lucifer, and the Tempter. If Satan could stop Jesus from accomplishing His mission, it would mean disaster for all mankind, and he knew it. If Jesus sinned, that would cause Him to fall from His perfect and sinless state. If He sinned, His mission failed.

Satan knows a great deal about each of us—our talents, future responsibilities, our weaknesses, and doubts. This knowledge prompts Him to strike just when important events are about to happen. He knew perfectly who Jesus was and that He was about to enter the world's stage as the Messiah.

How It Applies to Me

Know Your Enemy

Each of us needs to recognize and believe that the devil is real and that he is actively trying to harm us. "Know your enemy," as they say in the military.

He is often called the father of lies. And he *hates* you. And he hates me too. (See John 8:44.) Every day, his sole purpose and intention is to ruin our glorious opportunities for spiritual growth by deceiving and enticing us to do harmful, destructive things.

His favorite lies are: "There is no devil" and "You can get away with that—no consequences." That's like an enemy telling a group of soldiers, "There are no mines on that road. You can drive on it, no problem." Then the soldiers' vehicles get blown to the sky as the enemy laughs and cheers.

The Devil and his followers can *influence* our thinking—but they can't *control* it until we listen to them. They can use other people, the Internet, magazines, art, music, or any other source to plant thoughts and evil desires, but it's up to us whether we make the choices they prompt us to make.

As the "enemy of all righteousness," Satan wants to stop us from believing in Jesus, the "fountain of all righteousness." (See Acts 13:10.) By influencing us to take Jesus and His gospel lightly—or reject Him—Satan wins the war. We then fail in our mission to embrace all that is good and reject all that is evil.

The First Temptation—Food

In the New Testament story of Jesus, we read of three specific temptations. From these, we can learn much about how to overcome temptation ourselves.

Because He possessed godly powers, He could do things that were impossible for man—like fasting for forty days.

Jesus's mother, however, was Mary. Therefore, He also endured the weaknesses and pains that we all have as humans. Imagine forty days without food. At this moment of physical weakness, his uninvited guest showed up:

> *And when he had fasted forty days and forty nights, he was afterward an hungred [hungry].*
>
> *And when the tempter came to him, he said, "If thou be the Son of God, command that these stones be made bread."*
>
> *But he answered and said, "It is written, Man shall not live by bread alone, but by every word that proceedeth out of the mouth of God."* (Matthew 4:2-4)

Whether the Devil actually spoke the words to Jesus or simply "whispered" this thought into Jesus's mind, we do not know.

Was this temptation only about food? Did you notice the Devil's first word? "*If* thou be the Son of God," he said. Perhaps the Devil was playing up Jesus's possible doubts about who He really was, tempting Jesus to "test drive" His miraculous powers.

Up to this point, Jesus had not performed any miracles that we know of. But was it appropriate to prove to Himself that He could do it? Snap His fingers and presto—a loaf of bread to satisfy His own hunger? With this single, sneaky suggestion, the Devil tried to pull at Jesus from different directions.

But was Jesus really pulled at all? He likely saw through the ploy in an instant. Was He even *capable* of sinning? Yes, absolutely He was. He could have chosen to sin at any time in His life. He had the freedom and power to choose, as we all do. Apostle Paul taught that Jesus "was in all points tempted like as we are, yet without sin" (Hebrews 4:15).

How did Jesus brush off the tempter's suggestion? With a scripture. Life is much more than bread, He said. Real life comes by the word of God—by following every word. Jesus was determined to follow the will of His Father, rather than satisfy His hunger or test out His powers.

Doctrinal Points to Ponder

How Much Did Jesus Know?

Was Jesus an all-knowing God even as a child? Did He have a complete and perfect understanding of His mission at the time He experienced these temptations?

It appears that the answer to both questions is "no" and that Jesus passed into this earthly life as we all did. He grew line upon line, choosing to believe, act wisely, and develop faith—as we all must. (See Hebrews 5:8.)[17]

This is important because it makes Jesus's example to us even more inspiring. Truly, God Himself, the very Creator, showed us the way in every respect, including how to develop faith and demonstrate obedience based on an incomplete but growing spiritual knowledge. Of course, He did it perfectly and far more effectively and rapidly than any man, but He did it nonetheless. Praise be to God in the highest, indeed.

The Second Temptation—a Sign from God

Having lost the first round, Satan moved on to plan B:

> *Then the devil taketh him up into the holy city, and setteth him on a pinnacle of the temple.*
>
> *And saith unto him, "If thou be the Son of God, cast thyself down: for it is written, He shall give his angels charge concerning thee: and in their hands they shall bear thee up, lest at any time thou dash thy foot against a stone."*
>
> *Jesus said unto him, "It is written again, Thou shalt not tempt the Lord thy God." (Matthew 4:5-7)*

The Devil does not have power to physically transport us wherever he wants only to launch temptations in our face. Perhaps Jesus was already at the temple, or the Devil planted this image in Jesus's mind and He imagined Himself atop the highest point.

Look at all of the trickery folded into this second temptation. The Devil made his suggestion appear legitimate by first quoting scripture. He twisted the meaning of the scripture to be sure, implying that it would be okay for Jesus to demand that His Father provide a miracle to save Him from a death plunge. Again, there is the word "if," hoping to trigger more doubts that He really is the Christ.

And what about fame and recognition? What had Jesus been praying for during the last forty days? He was preparing to go among the people, hoping to bless their lives. What if all people near the temple looked up and witnessed an event like this, where the angels of heaven swooped down to save this man, Jesus, from Nazareth, as He fell from the pinnacle of the temple? How quickly would they embrace Him as the Christ and accept His teachings? That's real temptation.

The Third Temptation—All Worldly Power and Glory

Satan's last attempt to derail the Lord's mission was almost beyond belief, nothing subtle about it. He laid it all on the table:

> *Again, the devil taketh him up into an exceeding high mountain, and sheweth him all the kingdoms of the world, and the glory of them;*
>
> *And saith unto him, "All these things will I give thee, if thou wilt fall down and worship me."*
>
> *Then saith Jesus unto him, "Get thee hence, Satan: for it is written, Thou shalt worship the Lord thy God, and him only shalt thou serve."*
>
> *Then the devil leaveth him, and, behold, angels came and ministered unto him. (Matthew 4:8–11)*

Satan tried to draw out any lust for power, wealth, or worldly fame that might have existed in Jesus's heart. He demanded that Jesus worship *him*. But Jesus's perfect heart, which loved only His Father and all that is good, brushed the Devil aside, again with scripture.

On His own authority, Jesus directed the Devil to leave Him. And by the authority of Jesus Christ, the Devil had to obey. To this day, it is through the authority and name of Jesus Christ that each of us can command Satan to leave us. And leave us he must.

His Life and Mine

What did Jesus do?

- When preparing for an important event, Jesus removed Himself from the distractions of ordinary life so He could fully focus on communicating with God.
- Jesus fasted, which increased the sensitivity of His Spirit.

- Jesus dismissed each temptation *immediately*. He didn't hesitate, imagining how pleasing it might be.
- Jesus knew that the Devil was real and drove Him away. He used scriptures to recognize temptations and knock them out of His way.

What would I do?

- When I'm wrestling with an important decision, do I fast to help me receive the guidance I need?
- Do I really believe there is an evil force in the world trying to influence us to make bad decisions—both in person and online? Can I become better at recognizing evil when it's around me and influencing me?
- Have I learned to recognize Satan's tactics? Do I know when he is pulling and prying at my personal weaknesses and lusts?
- Beginning right now, if I were to watch for the first temptation that enters my mind, would I let it mull around and tease me? Or would I immediately dismiss it?
- When beset with darkness and Satan's influence, have I ever said, "Satan, in the name of Jesus Christ, get away from me," and then cited a scripture or the words of a hymn, like Jesus did? Try it. It truly works.

Part Two

I Am the Messiah

Love from Above

Many believed in his name, when they saw the miracles which he did.

—John 2:23

My Upward Climb

Have I made the choice yet to believe in Jesus in an active, daily, intentional way?

Chapter 5

The Beginning of Miracles

Jumping off the pinnacle of the temple and being saved by an army of angels would have gone viral, no doubt, but the Devil's ways are not the Lord's ways. So, in what way did Jesus intend to make Himself known as the Messiah?

After Jesus was baptized and fasted in the wilderness, John the Baptist continued teaching that the Messiah was already among the people. Who could hear this and not be insanely curious? Many people took John very seriously, so the rumors, questions, and excitement about the Messiah were likely spreading throughout all Israel.

Gathering Disciples

It has been several weeks since Jesus was baptized and secluded Himself in the wilderness. Upon His return, Jesus's first step in making Himself known to the world was to gather followers who would witness everything He did. These followers became known as His disciples, meaning "those who seek to learn and follow."

Once again, look and envision John the Baptist teaching near the banks of the river, surrounded by a typical crowd of his own disciples plus seekers and skeptics. John is continuing to teach, prepare, and cleanse the people through baptism.

At one point, John glances sharply at a spot in the crowd as he observes Jesus walking closer. *See, there He is.* John immediately recognizes an opportunity to fulfill his very mission. He points Jesus out to the people by crying, "Behold the Lamb of God!" (John 1:36)

All heads turn in the direction of John's gesture. It's possible that none of John's disciples know Jesus by sight at this time. And perhaps some had not even heard of Him. But the phrase, "Lamb of God," has an unmistakable meaning. "He is the Messiah," John is saying, the Messiah, standing before them in the flesh!

Making Sense of Scripture

Behold What?

When John the Baptist said, "Behold, the Lamb of God!" it meant a lot more than just saying, "There's the Lamb of God."

The word "behold" is one of those really rich words that people back then understood in a way we can't really appreciate today. Consider this insightful explanation by Bible translators who struggled with how to render the original word:

"The word 'behold' means something like 'Pay careful attention to what follows! This is important!' Other than the word 'behold,' there is no single word in English that fits well in most contexts. Although 'Look!' and 'See!' and 'Listen!' would be workable in some contexts, in many others these words lack sufficient weight and dignity."[18]

Wouldn't John the Baptist use the absolute strongest language, with all possible weight and dignity to get the people's attention? Yes, and he certainly did.

Two of the Baptist's close followers (Andrew and a different man named John) immediately approach Jesus. They appear very excited as they approach. Jesus turns to them and kindly asks, "What do you want?" (John 1:38, NIV) They answer with a question:

> *They said, "Rabbi" (which means "Teacher"), "where are you staying?" (John 1:38, NIV)*

Note the great respect they show by calling Him Rabbi. Jesus replies, "Come and see." So they walk away, following Jesus, hearing Him for the first time. Imagine the feelings of their hearts as they search His eyes and consider His words, remembering the strong witness of John the Baptist. Incredibly, they are walking with the Messiah.

Soon after, Andrew is so excited about finding Jesus that the first thing he does is quickly find his brother Simon:

> *He first findeth his own brother Simon, and saith unto him, "We have found the Messias," which is, being interpreted, the Christ.*
>
> *And he brought him to Jesus. And when Jesus beheld him, he said, "Thou art Simon the son of Jona: thou shalt be called Cephas," which is by interpretation, A stone. (John 1:41-42)*

Clearly, Andrew took John the Baptist's witness wholly to heart.

As soon as Jesus met Simon, he gave him a new name: He called him Cephas, which also means stone or rock. The name Peter also means rock. Most often, the scriptures refer to this man as Peter, not Simon, but sometimes we see both names together as Simon Peter. He is mentioned more often than any other disciple and plays an extremely important role later in the New Testament.

Superhuman Knowledge

Peter had never even seen Jesus prior to that meeting. Could the Master know of things long before they even happened? Could He discern a man's heart by just looking at him?

Watch what happens when Jesus finds two more disciples. He tells one of them, Nathanael, that He has already seen him and then shares something very private that only Nathanael would know:

> *Jesus saw Nathanael coming to him, and saith of him, "Behold an Israelite indeed, in whom is no guile!"*

> *Nathanael saith unto him, "Whence knowest thou me?" Jesus answered and said unto him, "Before that Philip called thee, when thou wast under the fig tree, I saw thee."*
>
> *Nathanael answered and saith unto him, "Rabbi, thou art the Son of God; thou art the King of Israel."*
>
> *Jesus answered and said unto him, "Because I said unto thee, I saw thee under the fig tree, believest thou? Thou shalt see greater things than these." (John 1:47-50)*

To Nathanael, this was witness enough. The Savior told him two things no ordinary man could have known. First, although He had never met him, Jesus perceived that the man's heart has "no guile" (meaning he's not deceptive or sneaky). Second, Jesus had seen Nathanael under a fig tree. Perhaps he had been praying about something very personal or doing something that he was sure nobody could see while he was near a certain fig tree. Yet Jesus knew it perfectly and told him that He had seen him there. Nathanael was stunned. He immediately worshipped Him as the Son of God.

Jesus has so far met Andrew, John, Peter, Philip, and Nathanael. Shortly after, He found John in his fishing boat with his brother James. He called for them to leave and follow Him, which they immediately did.

Each of them managed to leave their business affairs to others and trust in Jesus, following Him day after day. Let's not forget that these were ordinary men with families (most likely), jobs, and dreams. In a sense, they were as average as any man that ever lived. But they were not ordinary men. In spirit, they were among the most faithful and courageous breed of men the world has ever known. Most end up paying the ultimate price, being tortured and murdered.

The Lord didn't just bump into them by chance; He had gone hunting. Much later, Jesus would tell these men:

> *"Ye have not chosen me, but I have chosen you, and ordained you, that ye should go and bring forth fruit." (John 15:16)*

It appears that the Master had a purpose in finding these men before He started His work. As far as we know, He did not perform a single miracle until this small group of disciples could be there to witness it.

The Marriage Feast at Cana

Sometime after Jesus gathered this small group of disciples, we find them together at a large marriage feast. All is enjoyable until a small crisis occurs.

Jesus's mother is there and approaches Him somewhat frantically, telling Him that there is no wine left. It looks like she is coordinating the event, or at least she feels responsible to help. In those days, everyone drank wine with dinner, especially at a wedding. Guests expected it to be there, and it would be embarrassing if you ran out.

Mary knows that Jesus is not an ordinary son to her. She may have hinted or come right out and asked Jesus to use His divine power to help her. We don't know. Nevertheless, believing that Jesus can help in some way—with or without a miracle—she directs some servants, "Whatsoever He saith unto you, do it" (John 2:5).

Of course, Jesus dearly loves His mother. Can you see the Lord's kindly eyes and calm smile to soften her concerns? His new little group of disciples is with Him too, watching all that He does and how He carries Himself. In every situation, great and small, He is their leader. In His wisdom, He determines that it is appropriate to solve the problem in an astonishing way.

The First Miracle

Jesus walks over to His mother's servants and directs them to fill six large pots with water, which is not easy without modern faucets. The pots hold nearly twenty-five gallons each—totaling roughly 150 gallons.[19] This must be a *big* wedding.

Then Jesus directs one of the servants to "Draw out now, and bear unto the governor of the feast" (John 2:8). The servant likely wondered and hesitated at such a command, knowing the pot had just been filled with ordinary well water.

Obediently, the servant dips a cup into one of the pots and—perhaps with doubtful, trembling hands—serves it to the governor of the feast, but it is wine. In fact, the governor says to the groom, "Every man at the beginning doth set forth good wine; and when men have well drunk, then that which is worse: but thou hast kept the good wine until now" (John 2:10).

The guests are thrilled. It seems they saved the best for last!

How It Applies to Me

The Savior and Social Gatherings

At this wedding and many other social gatherings in the future, we'll find the Savior and His disciples having a nice time, interacting with people, and enjoying rest and relaxation. Of course, there are opportunities to teach, serve, or comfort others, but it's clear that Jesus approved of appropriate entertainment.[20]

This is just one example where Jesus showed us that it's possible to live within the normal flow of life and attend appropriate social events, yet maintain a high standard of behavior.

The servants, who had perfect knowledge of what just occurred, could have been incredibly excited and amazed by this, telling everyone they knew what had just happened (unless Jesus specifically directed them not to tell anyone—which He did from time to time).

Jesus typically performed miracles only when the people present had at least *some* belief or hope for God's power. For Peter, Andrew, John, and the other disciples, this was an important event that rewarded and strengthened their faith in Him, but this was nothing compared to what lay ahead.

Making Sense of Scripture

Faith in the Lord Jesus Christ

While miracles may fascinate us and tickle our curiosity for a while, they don't change us. In and of themselves, they don't bring us to the "joyous life" described in the very beginning of this book. Consider this important statement by author John MacArthur:

"What does it mean to believe in Christ? It means more than accepting and affirming the truth of who He is—God in human flesh—and believing what He says. Real faith has at its heart a willingness to obey."[21]

Soon, you will hear Jesus describe Himself as Living Water. He will promise us salvation when we drink the Living Water. When we drink something, we take it deep inside, and it becomes part of us. When we drink, we commit. If we drink poison, we've committed to the consequences. If we drink a life-saving medication, we will be saved by its powerful effect. Sniffing it, looking at it, and believing that it might help won't save us.

To understand the scriptures correctly, we must understand that the phrase "believe on the name of Jesus" implicitly assumes a willingness—even an intention—to trust, to honor, to worship, and to obey Him.

His Life and Mine

What did Jesus do?

- Jesus remembered His purpose and mission at all times, without getting caught up in worldly distractions.
- Jesus's first known miracle was an act of kindness to resolve a small matter that some might have considered unworthy of the attention of the Lord of hosts.
- Jesus began nurturing and preparing his future apostles from their first day together.
- When people craved answers and leadership, Jesus was willing to step up and provide it. He was willing to say, in effect, "Watch me and follow me."

What would I do?

- Am I staying focused on what God wants me to do with my life, just like Jesus stayed focused on His mission?
- Have I ever heard a little "voice" tell me that I'm spending too much time on social media? That it's interfering with more important things?
- When a family member asks for my help with something small, will I remember Jesus's example and cheerfully assist?
- Do I realize that people are watching my behavior at school, at home, or at work?
- Maybe I have friends who need a leader and a good example—someone like me. Can I take them under my wing and express my faith in them? My praise and attention might pump them with energy and motivate their best selves.

Love from Above

Whoever has the Son has life; whoever does not have the Son of God does not have life.

—1 John 5:12, NIV

My Upward Climb

Have I told Heavenly Father all of the ways that Jesus has inspired me, taught me, and blessed me?

(If you're still on the fence about Jesus, that's okay. Perhaps you can ask God to help you understand why it's important to believe in Him or in spiritual things in general.)

Chapter 6

My Father's House

Sometime after the wedding feast and the miracle of turning water into wine, Jesus and his small band of followers made their way to Jerusalem for the magnificent feast of the Passover.

Now things really heat up. It will be clear that Jesus has no problem asserting Himself. He understands who He is, and He will never act otherwise.

Jerusalem and the Passover

Jews at this time were scattered among many different countries, and they traveled long distances to attend Passover. The Jewish historian Josephus estimated the number of visitors to Jerusalem at about three *million*. Others say it was just one million. Even one million is about fifteen football stadiums full. That's a *lot* of people in an ancient city threaded with dozens of narrow streets.

John Cunningham Geikie, a well-respected Bible scholar, described it like this:

> *The streets were blocked by the crowds from all parts, who had to make their way to the temple past flocks of sheep and droves of cattle … Sellers of all possible items harassed the visitors … Inside the temple, the noise and pressure were, if possible, worse. The outer court was in part covered with pens for sheep, goats, and cattle, for the [sacrifices]. Sellers shouted the merits of their beasts, sheep bleated, and oxen lowed. It was, in fact, the great yearly fair of Jerusalem.*[22]

It was deafening and irreverent. It might have been exciting as a visitor or eager merchant. But the temple was the house of the Lord. Can you imagine such a scene outside *and inside* one of our church sanctuaries today? Imagine a group of pastors or bishops, or even the pope standing by and just watching all of this happen. But it's even worse than that. The scholar continued, "The sale of doves was, in great measure, secretly in the hands of the priests themselves: Hannas, the high priest, especially, gained great profits from his doves."[23]

The Jewish leaders of the day—the priests—were actually demanding higher than usual prices for animals to sacrifice—the very priests responsible to lead the people in righteousness.

By this time, Jesus had probably been to Passover nearly twenty times. The conditions were probably similar every year. No doubt His heart had been sickened before, but the time to begin His ministry had not yet come. So He had endured it—until now.

Jesus Cleanses the Temple

Watch now as Jesus slowly enters the temple amidst the chaos, walking this way and that, eyeing the priests. He turns to the money exchangers and watches them greedily cheating foreign visitors out of their meager coinage. He looks down, closing His eyes, deeply troubled by the noise and disrespect.

Jesus is just one among an enormous crowd. But He is the Lord God of Israel, and this is His Father's house.

We watch as Jesus gathers some bits of rope or leather strips and begins tying them together into a sort of whip. And then with complete authority, he begins commanding the people around Him, sweeping that holy place clean from one end to the other:

> *And when he had made a scourge of small cords, he drove them all out of the temple, and the sheep, and the oxen; and poured out the changers' money, and overthrew the tables;*
>
> *And said unto them that sold doves, "Take these things hence; make not my Father's house an house of merchandise." (John 2:15-16)*

Single-handedly, the Lord physically drives them all out. What a scene: animals scurrying away and people crawling to recover their coins as they rolled under the feet of men and beasts. People watching are drop-jawed, wide-eyed, astonished. Most people have no idea who Jesus is.

So why does anyone listen? We don't read that Jesus *tried* to cleanse the temple. He did cleanse the temple. How can a single, unknown person accomplish such a thing?

Jesus drove them out with the majesty of His presence and the strength that comes from standing up for what is right. The power to resist withers under a consciousness of guilt. In a world where "might makes right," here we see an example of "right makes might."[24]

You can imagine the impression this makes on the people who watch this happen, seeing the Jewish leaders powerless to stop Him. Recall that the people generally feared the Jewish leaders and expected them to have the last word. But not this time.

The Jewish Leaders Question Jesus

After the confusion dies down, the Jewish leaders approach Jesus, bristling and furious.

> *"What sign shewest thou unto us, seeing that thou doest these things?" (John 2:18)*

Notice that they don't question whether His actions were right. No, they question why He should be the one to do what was really *their* job. In effect, they are asking, "What gives you the authority to do this?"

Jesus's answer seems strange: "Destroy this temple and in three days I will raise it up." The scriptures tell us that, "He spake of the temple of His body" (John 2:18–21). This is actually Jesus's first prediction that His body (His temple) would die and rise again on the third day.

At first the Jews think He is speaking of the actual temple building. This is laughable to them, so they scoff at Jesus, "Forty and six years was this temple in building, and wilt thou rear it up in three days?" (John 2:20).

Later we'll see that they never forgot these words and held it against Him to the end. They must have eventually figured out the meaning, however, because during His trial and crucifixion, they referred back to these very words, warning that He promised to rise again after three days.[25] (See Matthew 27:63.)

I *Am* the Messiah

The clearing of the temple represents Jesus's dramatic entrance onto the world stage as the Messiah. Does this story make you look at Jesus a little differently? Watch for this theme throughout His life: He is the God of the whole earth and He will always act like it. If you have ever wondered what God would do if He Himself were here on earth, read on. You're holding the answer in your hands.

His Life and Mine

What did Jesus do?

- Jesus took decisive action against the disgrace in the temple. He was bold and fearless, dynamic and powerful.
- Jesus showed us it is important to be reverent, to show respect unto God, and keep sacred things sacred.

What would you do?

- Consider your bedroom, apartment, or home. Is it like the temple that Jesus cleared out? What would Jesus think of how you keep your surroundings? Have you made it a place to uplift you or is it full of worldly or filthy things? Pictures of Jesus, sacred buildings, beautiful scenes of nature, and family memories can make it more sacred.

- Perhaps you're a parent who wants to make your home a place where the Spirit of God can be felt, where children learn and grow in the things of eternity. You're troubled by the types of TV, Internet, smartphone, and video game entertainment that's polluting your home. Whether you're a parent or child, should you let it go on? Can you find motivation from Jesus's example? Without becoming a self-righteous tornado, are there ways to clean your family's sacred place?
- Is your life too consumed by music? If your mind and heart are *your* temple, is it like the temple Jesus cleared out because it's so full of distraction and noise? Would Jesus be comfortable coming into your temple, or are there always headphones plugged into it?

Love from Above

"If any man thirst, let him come unto me, and drink.

"He that believeth on me, as the scripture hath said, out of his belly shall flow rivers of living water."

—John 7:37–38

My Upward Climb

Have I noticed a satisfying, peaceful sensation as I study and believe in Jesus with all my heart?

Chapter 7

The Woman of Samaria

After the Passover and the cleansing of the temple, Jesus and His disciples left Jerusalem to return to their homes up north, to the region of Galilee. To get there, most Jews would avoid an area between Jerusalem and Galilee called Samaria, preferring to travel around it.

Why avoid Samaria? The Jews *despised* Samaria because the inhabitants were a mixed race, partially of Israel and partly of Assyria and other nations (and therefore Gentiles). The Jews hated the Samaritans so much that they wouldn't even touch them or walk through their land—and the hatred was mutual. To call someone a Samaritan was a terrible insult.[26]

Jesus paid no attention to the prejudices against those people, so He walked with His disciples directly through Samaria. Once they arrived in Samaria, Jesus stopped to rest at an important landmark—Jacob's well. It was the original well dug by old father Jacob (Israel)—

the father of the twelve tribes—over one thousand years earlier, and it was still in use at the time Jesus arrived.

Look and see Jesus sitting alone by the well while His disciples are away looking for food. From a distance, He notices a Samaritan woman approaching slowly with an empty water pot. He who knows all things sits and waits until she arrives. He knows her life, her family, her thoughts, her spiritual longings, and her faith.

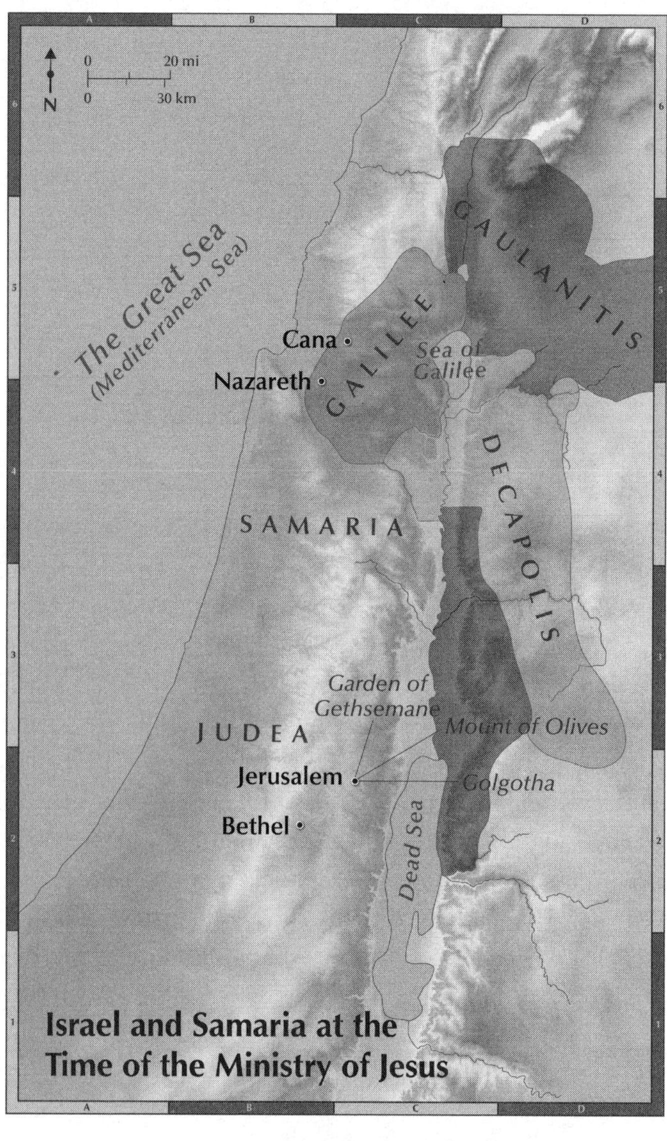

Israel and Samaria at the Time of the Ministry of Jesus

The woman sets her pot down near the well and leans over to start this frequent chore. Drawing water from the deep, old well isn't easy. The buckets and pots are heavy, and it takes a long time and some sweat to do it. Nevertheless:

> *Jesus saith unto her, "Give me to drink." [For his disciples were gone away unto the city to buy meat.]*
>
> *Then saith the woman of Samaria unto him, "How is it that thou, being a Jew, askest drink of me, which am a woman of Samaria? for the Jews have no dealings with the Samaritans." (John 4:7-9)*

She must be noticing that He is Jewish by His clothes or the way He talks. And she's shocked that He even speaks to her. But imagine His reassuring expression, perhaps with a gentle smile, and His friendly, confident voice.

> *Jesus answered and said unto her:*
>
> *"If thou knewest the gift of God, and who it is that saith to thee, Give me to drink; thou wouldest have asked of him, and he would have given thee living water."*
>
> *The woman saith unto him, "Sir, thou hast nothing to draw with, and the well is deep: from whence then hast thou that living water?" (John 4:10-11)*

She is of course thinking about the water in the well, but Jesus continues speaking symbolically, referring to the spiritual, living water that only He can give.

> *Jesus answered and said unto her:*
>
> *"Whosoever drinketh of this water shall thirst again:*
>
> *But whosoever drinketh of the water that I shall give him shall never thirst; but the water that I shall give him shall be in him a well of water springing up into everlasting life." (John 4:13-14)*

At this point, she might believe Jesus is offering her some "magic" water. Or is she beginning to perceive a spiritual meaning?

The woman saith unto him, "Sir, give me this water, that I thirst not, neither come hither to draw."

Jesus saith unto her, "Go, call thy husband, and come hither."

The woman answered and said, "I have no husband."

Jesus said unto her, "Thou hast well said, I have no husband:

For thou hast had five husbands; and he whom thou now hast is not thy husband: in that saidst thou truly."

The woman saith unto him, "Sir, I perceive that thou art a prophet." (John 4:15-19)

Prompted by Jesus's remarkable knowledge of her personal life, she recognizes that He is a prophet. She then makes a spiritual statement herself and receives a monumental response:

The woman saith unto him, "I know that Messias cometh, which is called Christ: when he is come, he will tell us all things."

Jesus saith unto her, "I that speak unto thee am he." (John 4:25-26)

Imagine the moment, the look in her eyes. Jesus tells her straight out that He is the Christ—sitting right in front of her. He sits silently, meeting her eyes, affirming the powerful impression that begins to fill her. This good woman immediately believes Him and excitedly runs back to the town, saying:

"Come, see a man, which told me all things that ever I did: is not this the Christ?" (John 4:29)

Jesus stayed there for two days, teaching all of the townspeople.

And many more believed because of his own word;

And said unto the woman, "Now we believe, not because of thy saying: for we have heard him ourselves, and know that this is indeed the Christ, the Savior of the world." (John 4:41-42)

These humble people listened carefully with open minds and hearts for two days and came to this knowledge for themselves: Jesus of Nazareth is the Savior of the world. How wonderful it would be to have a transcript of all that was spoken during those two days.

How It Applies to Me

Spiritual Understanding Takes Time

In some places, rain doesn't fall very often. Perhaps you've seen hard-baked ground that hasn't seen a drop of rain for months. I recall trying to drive a small garden stake into the ground in my backyard one time during a drought. I actually had to use a large hammer and a spike.

As we walk with Jesus, we will hear Him teach some things that will not be easy for us to understand—just like the Samaritan woman. His living water may flow right over us, like a flood of rain streaming over hard-baked earth without much of it sinking in at first.

Some doctrines (spiritual truths) take time to sink in. That's one reason we read the scriptures over and over again. The more spiritual we become, the more we can absorb. Like a garden that is cultivated over many years, our hearts become softer and more penetrable to the living water. Without that water, nothing grows.

True Worship and Organized Religion

Let's look at two more things that Jesus discussed with the woman of Samaria, starting with her question about where to worship. Her people had a tradition that was different than the Jewish tradition. "Who's right?" she basically asked.

> *"Our fathers worshipped in this mountain; and ye say, that in Jerusalem is the place where men ought to worship."*
>
> *Jesus saith unto her, "Woman, believe me, the hour cometh, when ye shall neither in this mountain, nor yet at Jerusalem, worship the Father.*
>
> *"Ye worship ye know not what: we know what we worship: for salvation is of the Jews." (John 4:20–22)*

This last statement is important: "We know what we worship: for salvation is of the Jews." Jesus made clear that the Jewish religion had the correct understanding of who God is and what is required to be saved (salvation). Even though Jesus knew most of the Jewish leaders were corrupt, He defended the teachings of their religion as a whole, as well as their priesthood authority to act in the name of God:

> *"But the hour cometh, and now is, when the true worshippers shall worship the Father in spirit and in truth: for the Father seeketh such to worship him." (John 4:23)*

God desires our sincere intentions and honesty in all we do. (See also Luke 8:15.) Jesus often taught the importance of being honest through such words as "true" and "pure." Hiding our sins, pretending to be something we are not, and clinging to false beliefs because they justify our actions—all of these are an offense and repulsive to the God of truth.

To Gather or Not to Gather: That Is the Question

There are some today who teach that Jesus preached against organized religion. They teach that people can just worship God in their heart and that He doesn't expect us to gather together as a group.

It is true that Jesus spoke out against people who twisted religious teachings. And He certainly pointed out hypocrisy when He saw it. He frequently condemned manmade changes to the commandments of God. But none of those things justify the view that Jesus was anti-organized religion.

We'll soon see that Jesus created an organization Himself with authorized servants. He even commanded them to go into the world and establish what would become the Christian church.

For many wise purposes, God commands us to meet together often as brothers and sisters in His kingdom. Jesus clearly believed in and supported the idea of religion as a well-structured, orderly body to learn from each other, serve each other, and grow together. Why else would He have said that the Jewish religion was correct and of God? Why else would He have started an organization and commanded them to carry on after He died if it was not important? (See Ephesians 4:11–12.)

How It Applies to Me

Glowing Ember or Dying Out?

A story is told of a man who had stopped coming to church because he was offended by the minister and others in the congregation. His best friend was concerned and visited with him, sitting together next to the warmth of the angry man's fireplace.

Nothing the friend could say would persuade him to come back. That "no-good minister" and "so-and-so gossipers" were more than he could stand, and he would not set another foot in that church, the man told him.

The friend then had an idea for the perfect analogy. He took the fireplace prongs and grabbed a large, orange, glowing ember and sat it on one of the bricks furthest from the rest of the embers.

"What are you doing?" the man asked.

"The same thing that you're doing," his friend replied.

Intrigued, the man watched as the ember grew darker and darker, until the faintest bit of orange had vanished. It had died out.

"I love you, and I want you to come back," pleaded the friend. "We embers need each other. Look what can happen when we separate ourselves from the church, the body of Christ."

The man sat in silence, understanding this simple truth in a way he had not considered before.

His Life and Mine

What did Jesus do?

- Jesus looked beyond prejudice, ignored foolish traditions, and loved everyone as children of God.
- Some of the Samaritans' beliefs were incorrect, and He told them so. The truth was found in the Jewish religion despite the wickedness of the leaders. He made clear that when teachings contradict each other, they can't all be correct.
- Jesus attended synagogue weekly, worshipped with others, and taught others to do the same.

What would I do?

- Imagine a friend at your work or school is of a different race or has some mental issues. Some people go out of their way not to get involved, or they make fun of her. Do I also walk around her, or will I see her as a sister and child of God with needs, hopes, and feelings like me?
- At a church or family gathering, I find myself with a choice between spending time with "the fun people" who seem to have little or no problems and sitting with a troubled (and perhaps annoying or difficult) person or family who needs a real lift and a friendly word. What do I do?
- When I stay in bed instead of going to church, thinking, "I'll just pray and have a sincere, worshipful heart this week," is this consistent with the Savior's example and teaching?
- Perhaps you know someone who says you're being a bigot if you claim to know what is true regarding Christ and His teachings. If I have a testimony of certain truths, will I speak up respectfully and confidently?

Love from Above

"Now we believe, not because of thy saying: for we have heard him ourselves, and know that this is indeed the Christ, the Savior of the world."

—John 4:42

My Upward Climb

Do the words and stories of Jesus fill me with light, understanding, gratitude, and feelings of worship?

If not, have I tried consciously, actively believing on His name and doing this repeatedly and consistently, understanding that light may come in trickles and small streams at first?

Chapter 8

Rejected by His Own

After their short stay in Samaria, Jesus and His small group of disciples continued traveling north to their home region of Galilee. As the news of Jesus spread, more and more people came out to see this new Prophet as He walked by. We read:

> *Jesus returned in the power of the Spirit into Galilee: and there went out a fame of him through all the region round about. (Luke 4:14)*

Return to Nazareth

Jesus eventually arrived back in Nazareth and attended synagogue on the Sabbath day "as his custom was" (Luke 4:16), with the townspeople He knew so well. These were the folks who watched Him grow up. They probably treated Him kindly as a boy and helped His family with various needs. Some of those present probably taught Him from the scriptures and the law. Jesus likely served many of them as a craftsman along with His stepfather, Joseph, and His half-brothers.

They no doubt remembered Him as a "very good boy" and probably thought of Him with fondness and pride. But what did they think about Jesus now? Surely the rumors had reached them. They likely heard about Him clearing out the temple in Jerusalem. And surely they had heard stories of the healings which had begun taking place by this time. They probably wondered, "Does He really consider Himself a prophet?"

They're about to find out.

The Sabbath Meeting

See, now a large group of villagers seated in a building with benches along three walls and some seated on the floor.[27] During a Sabbath meeting, time is allowed for adults other than the rabbi to stand in front of the congregation, read a section of scripture, and teach from it.[28]

Today, after hearing the rabbi teach, Jesus stands and walks to the front to read. The man in charge smiles and hands Jesus a large roll of scripture. His townspeople are primed, and they listen very carefully. Jesus reads a section from the Old Testament, from the prophet Isaiah:

> *"The Spirit of the Lord is upon me, because he hath anointed me to preach the gospel to the poor; he hath sent me to heal the broken-hearted, to preach deliverance to the captives, and recovering of sight to the blind, to set at liberty them that are bruised, to preach the acceptable year of the Lord."*
>
> *And he closed the book, and he gave it again to the minister, and sat down. And the eyes of all them that were in the synagogue were fastened on him. (Luke 4:18–20; Isaiah 61:1–2)*

It's deathly quiet. Why are all eyes fastened on Him so?

Because the scripture Jesus just read is a classic, unmistakable verse that most everyone knows. It describes that great day when the Christ will come among His people.

Jesus's first words after sitting down are shocking to them as well, and there's no room for confusion here:

And he began to say unto them, "This day is this scripture fulfilled in your ears."

And all bare him witness, and wondered at the gracious words which proceeded out of his mouth. And they said, "Is not this Joseph's son?" (Luke 4:21-22)

And many hearing him were astonished, saying, "From whence hath this man these things and what wisdom is this which is given unto him, that even such mighty works are wrought by his hands?

"Is not this the carpenter, the son of Mary, the brother of James, and Joses, and of Juda, and Simon? And are not his sisters here with us?" And they were offended at him. (Mark 6:2-3)

No Honor in His Own Country

At first they "wondered at the gracious words," perhaps touched by His message and manner. (Jesus clearly said more than was captured in the New Testament, based on what is written above.) He appeared to have intrigued and even impressed them. But wonder soon turned into stunned silence and sideways glances. They began to doubt and boil in their thoughts: "How can Jesus possibly be the Messiah? This is the boy we watched grow up."

He who can read the thoughts of all people perceived a stubborn skepticism and perhaps even a desire to see proof—a miracle. Why wouldn't His hometown friends get to see some exciting exhibition of His power?[29] So Jesus responded to their thoughts and mumbled questions.

And He said, "Verily I say unto you, No prophet is accepted in his own country" (Luke 4:24).

He went on to remind them of two famous stories in the scriptures when certain Gentiles believed and obeyed Israelite prophets from faraway lands more than the Israelite people themselves. He was warning the people of Nazareth to beware that they should not make the same mistake.

Really? How dare He suggest that even the hated Gentiles were more righteous and believing than they? Outrageous. Here's what they thought of their "very good boy" now:

> *And all they in the synagogue, when they heard these things, were filled with wrath,*
>
> *And rose up, and thrust him out of the city, and led him unto the brow of the hill whereon their city was built, that they might cast him down headlong. (Luke 4:28–29)*

Jesus Is Attacked

Filled with murderous rage, His own townspeople physically grabbed Jesus and carried Him to the edge of a nearby cliff to throw Him over headfirst. Tragically, Jesus's immediate family members were likely there too, horrified by this mob of their own neighbors.[30]

The scriptures don't tell us how Jesus escaped. Either through a miracle or simply walking through the midst of the confused throng, we read that, "He passing through the midst of them went his way" (Luke 4:30).

The people of Nazareth needed to know their Savior as much as any of us. Jesus essentially told them, "I am the prophesied Messiah," but they failed to perceive His godly character and believe His witness.

How might you have responded to Jesus if you had grown up as one of his boyhood friends and been in the synagogue that day? That's a question worth considering. Would you have known the difference between a true Messenger from God and a deceiver with an inflated ego?[31] Would you seek guidance from God to know the truth, or would you rely on your own understanding?

Making Sense of Scripture

Misunderstandings About the Messiah

Recall that the Jews were taught that the Messiah would come as a powerful political king who would crush the nations who oppressed them, not as a humble craftsman.

Surely there was evidence that pointed to Jesus as the true Messiah. But did anybody know that angels sang to shepherds, announcing the Messiah's birth thirty years earlier? Very unlikely.

Did they know He was born in Bethlehem—as prophesied— and not in Nazareth? Perhaps some of his townspeople knew it, but most Jews did not, as we'll see later.

Without the benefit of internet or TV, were most people aware that John the Baptist had testified saying, "Behold, the Lamb of God"? Perhaps not.

There's an important insight in this: the truth is often declared in the midst of conflicting stories and perceptions, where people may not have all of the facts. It appears to be part of the plan and an intentional test of life. God expects us to love the truth enough to sift through it all and discern the evidence that really matters.

We must crave the knowledge of what is good and true, turning over every stone of evidence and asking God for guidance to find it. And find it we will, for so God has promised those who seek with an honest heart and are willing to do and change anything in their life when they find it.

Consider again the beautiful verse that Jesus read from the book of Isaiah. Does this sound like a nation-crushing Messiah or a merciful one who reaches down to humble individuals, teaching, healing, and delivering from sin, abuse, and addictions?

> *"The Spirit of the Lord is upon me, because he hath anointed me to preach the gospel to the poor; he hath sent me to heal the broken-hearted, to preach deliverance to the captives, and recovering of sight to the blind, to set at liberty them that are bruised." (Luke 4:18)*

His Life and Mine

What did Jesus do?

- Jesus focused on teaching, helping, and loving even when others watched Him scornfully and criticized Him unfairly.
- Jesus fulfilled His role even when the message was not easy to accept. He said it anyway, without fear or hesitation. The people of Nazareth did not want to believe Him, but that was their choice and their accountability.
- Jesus was terribly mistreated by people who knew Him well and should have behaved better.

What would I do?

- Do I desire to share the Gospel but have a tendency to not say anything to certain "types" of people? Am I concerned they will reject me? Can Jesus's example help? With appropriate tact, can I speak up while thinking, *I'll let them decide for themselves. Only God knows their heart*? (See 1 Samuel 16:7.)
- When facing a socially or physically intimidating situation, can Jesus's continual fearlessness embolden me, remembering that "God has not given us a spirit of fear, but of power and of love and of a sound mind" (2 Timothy 1:7, NKJV)?
- When my family or close friends do terrible things to me, can I draw strength from Jesus and remember His courage, knowing what the people of His hometown did to Him and yet He went on His way, doing good?

Love from Above

For as the body without the spirit is dead, so faith without works is dead also.

—James 2:26

My Upward Climb

Is seeing Jesus in action making it easier to believe in Him and to want to act like Him?

Do I understand that my belief in Jesus must lead to trust, which leads to a willingness to do as He does, to live as He lived?

Chapter 9
Healing and Forgiveness

Sometime early in Jesus's ministry, He traveled to Capernaum, a prosperous, busy town in the Galilee region. It was the home of Peter (Simon) and Andrew and a place Jesus and His disciples would visit often.

While participating in Sabbath services in Capernaum, a man possessed by an evil spirit suddenly began to be tossed about in the midst of the synagogue. What a bizarre and troubling scene. But today, Jesus was there and he promptly cast out the evil spirit. All eyes watched this mighty miracle unfold until the writhing man cried out, being "torn" by the spirit, and then he mysteriously and calmly settled into his right mind. (See Mark 1:26.) Of course, news of such a thing traveled as fast as feet could run.

And immediately his fame spread abroad throughout all the region round about Galilee. (Mark 1:28)

While the gossip press began publishing this story all over the city of Capernaum and beyond, Jesus and some of His disciples went to the home of the brothers, Peter and Andrew. Things weren't going very well when they arrived.

And forthwith, when they were come out of the synagogue, they entered into the house of Simon and Andrew, with James and John.

But Simon's wife's mother lay sick of a fever, and anon they tell him of her.

And he came and took her by the hand, and lifted her up; and immediately the fever left her, and she ministered unto them. (Mark 1:29-31)

If Peter and Andrew's family had any doubts about Jesus before, this healing would surely encourage them. Here we learn that Peter had a wife. He likely had children too. We may forget to think of Jesus's disciples as people with families who made real sacrifices to follow Jesus. Today's compassionate healing might be just the reassuring witness and reward this family needed.

An Entire City Healed

Inside, imagine a wooden table in the center of a single-room home with people seated on the floor around it, as was common at that time. Peter's mother-in-law is now completely well and helping with this and that in the house. The family enjoys listening to Jesus and hearing the disciples' stories of their travels. As the sun starts going down, they hear noises outside, and Peter looks out of a window in his home. There's a tide of people coming from every direction, some running. Someone must have spread the word that the new Prophet, Jesus of Nazareth, is in Peter's house.

At evening, when the sun had set, they brought to Him all who were sick and those who were demon-possessed.

And the whole city was gathered together at the door.

> *Then He healed many who were sick with various diseases, and cast out many demons; and He did not allow the demons to speak, because they knew Him. (Mark 1:32-34, NKJV)*

Even though the scripture says, "the whole city," surely there were some people who stayed at home. In Jewish tradition, it was common and acceptable to exaggerate the size of something to make a point. But given that Capernaum was a center of trade and commerce, lying at the intersection of important roads, this was probably a city of one thousand or more. So, "the whole city" had to represent *at least* several hundred people pouring into the streets and crowding around Peter's home.

Making Sense of Scripture

Envisioning Scriptural Events

Very short descriptions of events, like "He healed many who were sick with various diseases," are very common in the scriptures. It's worth stopping sometimes to envision what such events must have been like, rather than plowing forward thinking, "I get it. Jesus healed a lot of people."

Scriptural stories are full of deeply significant events that were life-changing and awe-inspiring to those who were there. A bit of reasonable envisioning—without purporting as fact—can make the experience more enriching.

The following segment includes details that are *not* part of the scriptural account but are here to illustrate the grandeur of this evening outside of Peter's home.

Imagine Peter looking at the growing crowd, astounded. Some of them look terribly weak, being carried or leaning on others. A young girl with a severely deformed face walks hand in hand with her father. An older woman is bent over and struggles to even look up as she walks, with people passing quickly around her. Several are clearly mentally ill or have distorted, angry faces, being tugged along by their family. Others look perfectly healthy, gathering in small groups to support the sick or to see what the new Prophet will do.

Peter turns to Jesus to describe what's happening. Jesus smiles, stands, and walks to the open door, still smiling gently. He knows He can help them. Some have suffered for years. Healing them is one way in which He is their Savior.

A ripple goes through the crowd as someone recognizes Him. Each family presses closer to the door. Jesus begins talking with those nearest to Him. He who knows the hearts and thoughts of all men senses that their faith is sufficient to be healed.

At the Master's word, the old woman stands straight up and free of pain for the first time in years. "Praise God," she cries out with arms raised, as she hugs everyone she knows.

The father of the deformed child takes courage and pleads with Jesus to help his daughter, knowing it will save her from a life of teasing and loneliness. With tenderness, Jesus passes His hand over her face as though removing a mask, showing her true identity—a cute little girl with an "I love you, Daddy" smile. The man is overcome and falls at the Master's feet.

The mentally ill and those possessed with devils are able to speak in their right minds—some for the first time in their lives as if awaking from a sleep—causing their mothers and fathers to weep with relief.

One by one He heals them. Peter and Andrew's family is there to witness it all from beginning to end. Eventually, the crowd separates, and the street becomes quiet and dark. This night is sealed into each person's memory.

Incredibly, scenes like this will become common as Jesus walks back and forth across the land of Israel for three years.

Lepers—The Walking Dead

Some days later, Jesus and His followers are walking in another area of Galilee. It's now common for large crowds to gather and walk with Him for a while. But suddenly, a frightening thing happens:

> *And it came to pass, when he was in a certain city, behold a man full of leprosy: who seeing Jesus fell on his face, and besought him, saying, "Lord, if thou wilt, thou canst make me clean." (Luke 5:12)*

The poor man kneeling before Jesus looks awful. Being "full of leprosy," his skin and hair are freakish, and his face looks like a Halloween mask. People nearby shrink back in horror, never having been so close to someone like this. Yet he falls near the feet of Jesus, who is completely unafraid.

People back then were terrified by leprosy, which is highly contagious. Today we can treat it with simple antibiotics, but in those days, it was a death sentence.

When you got the disease, your body slowly began to turn white at the tips of your fingers, toes, ears, etc. Your hair would turn a sick-looking yellow. Later, raw flesh would appear. Little pieces of your hands, feet, face, and even eyes would fall off while you were still alive. You knew you were going to die. You just watched yourself and others die this ugly, horrifying death.[32]

But this man has a new hope. It's the new Prophet. He calls out, "Lord, if thou wilt, thou canst make me clean," as if saying, "I know you can do it, but *will* you do it for me?"[33] Clearly, he believes in Jesus:

> *And Jesus, moved with compassion, put forth his hand, and touched him, and saith unto him, "I will; be thou clean." (Mark 1:41)*

As soon as Jesus reaches to touch him, all of the people gasp in disbelief and step back. *Nobody* touches a leper. But Jesus does exactly that, surrounded by a widening ring of astonished onlookers.

> *And as soon as he had spoken, immediately the leprosy departed from him, and he was cleansed.*
>
> *And he straitly charged him, and forthwith sent him away;*
>
> *And saith unto him, "See thou say nothing to any man: but go thy way, shew thyself to the priest, and offer for thy cleansing those things which Moses commanded, for a testimony unto them."*
>
> *But he went out, and began to publish it much, and to blaze abroad the matter, insomuch that Jesus could no more openly enter into the city, but was without in desert places: and they came to him from every quarter. (Luke 5:13–15)*

Before their eyes, this man's skin and hair return to normal, before their very eyes. Jesus was already famous, but now, the news "blazed abroad" that Jesus had healed the most dreaded disease—leprosy. It was the greatest of His miracles to this point, as far as we know.

Did you notice that Jesus told the man to go to the priest and do "those things which Moses commanded"? Again, Jesus was not anti-religion. He upheld the laws of God as revealed through His prophets. He had not come to tear down or criticize the law of Moses.

Why would He? It was He who gave the law to Moses.

Doctrinal Points to Ponder

Leprosy and Spiritual Death

The scriptures sometimes speak of "spiritual death." We certainly don't bury spirits, so what is spiritual death?

Let's look at the opposite—spiritual life. It's the kind of life that Jesus lived—loving what is true, doing only good, and being obedient to God. It's being completely free from the darkness and heaviness of sin.

When I sin, I am choosing darkness over light. The scriptures warn that if I continue in sin, my conscience will numb, and it will stop working. (See Ephesians 4:18–19.) My interest in doing good things begins to die. I feel far away from God and doubt He is even there. I also become less and less *able* to do good things. I am driven more and more by selfish behavior. I begin to feel alone, in the dark, and hopeless.

To get past the numb and empty feeling, I may seek the excitement of more serious, deeper sins, but eventually I only feel more emptiness and fear. It's a gripping spiral downward. There are usually temporary thrills and inappropriate fun with sin, but it never lasts, and it always ends in unhappiness.

Think of the most mean-spirited, selfish person you've ever known. Add some criminal behavior and some out-of-control addictions. Add a passion for lying and getting over on people. Assume he criticizes even the suggestion of being kind to people. This person is nearly dead spiritually. When we stand before God after our death, it is our spirit He will see, covered with filth and full of disease (figuratively speaking) if we have lived such a life.

Leprosy is a perfect analogy for spiritual death: it comes on slowly. Our healthy life slips away a piece at a time. It makes us ugly and undesirable. People may begin to avoid us. Without treatment or a miracle, it usually gets worse.

There is powerful symbolism here. The leper seemed hopeless. The beauty of this story is that *nobody* is hopeless, and Jesus Christ can save anyone from themselves and their past.

Through the Roof

Sometimes we have to be persistent and do unusual things to solve our problems. What comes next is both funny and inspiring.

On a certain day, we find Jesus teaching while standing in the middle of a large, crowded house. The crowd is spilling out into the street so that many can't even get close to the doorway.

Toward the back of the crowd, there's a group of men carrying a sick man on a stretcher. They look frustrated, obviously hoping to reach Jesus with their friend. Then one points to the roof.

They move to the rear of the house and manage to lift their sick friend, stretcher and all, up onto the roof. Like most houses in Israel, the roof is flat and made up of large tiles that are movable. With surprising boldness, they begin moving roof tiles to make a big opening in the ceiling.

Inside the room below, to everyone's amazement, down comes a stretcher with a sick man on it, right into the room. After a rush of mumbled comments from the crowd and perhaps a few chuckles at this brazen approach, the house becomes quiet. All eyes are on the Master.

> *And when He saw their faith, he said unto him, "Man, thy sins are forgiven thee."*
>
> *And the scribes and the Pharisees began to reason, saying, "Who is this which speaketh blasphemies? Who can forgive sins, but God alone?"*
>
> *But when Jesus perceived their thoughts, he answering said unto them, "What reason ye in your hearts?*

> *"Which is easier, to say, Thy sins be forgiven thee; or to say, Rise up and walk?" (Luke 5:20-23)*

An Arrogant Man or God Himself?

Here again, the Lord knows their silent thoughts against Him. No mortal man has the right to say another man's sins are forgiven—everyone knows that.

Jesus's statement left the people with one of two conclusions: (1) Jesus is just a regular man but is making Himself equal to God—which is outrageously inappropriate and punishable by death according to Jewish law at the time. Or (2) He is actually God. He could be insane, of course, but nobody could credibly accuse Him of that given all that He said and did.

Given this situation, wouldn't the honest seeker of truth at least *consider* the possibility that Jesus is the Messiah?

Here's how the scriptures tell it:

> *"But that ye may know that the Son of man hath power upon earth to forgive sins," (he said unto the sick of the palsy,) "I say unto thee, Arise, and take up thy couch, and go into thine house."*
>
> *And immediately he rose up before them, and took up that whereon he lay, and departed to his own house, glorifying God.*
>
> *And they were all amazed, and they glorified God, and were filled with fear, saying, "We have seen strange things to day." (Luke 5:24-26)*

How It Applies to Me

The Hope of Healing *and* Forgiveness

Here again, we can take real heart from the symbolism of all these stories: healing our body is a lot like healing our spirit.

God can and will heal and forgive us, based on our needs, faith, and sincere efforts, just like the determined leper and the sick man who stopped at nothing to reach the Savior. These are stories of incredible hope.

But let us not think that such gifts are handed out like cookies to a group of spoiled children—whether they say please or not. The Savior knew the hearts and the faith of those who humbly begged His help. We have responsibilities too. For example, consider this important quote from George Herbert:

"He that cannot forgive others breaks the bridge over which he must pass himself, for every man hath need to be forgiven."[34]

In Part Three, Jesus teaches what we must do in order to follow Him, to walk the path of recovery from our own spiritual diseases, and to enjoy the fullness of spiritual life with Him.

His Life and Mine

What did Jesus do?

- Jesus may have had a long day before the entire city came to Peter's door with their sick. Even though He was the Son of God, His body became tired just like the rest of us, but He served to the fullest.
- Jesus had compassion, even for people who are not attractive and whose lives are falling apart. He even reached out to the leper—someone who had been avoided "like the plague."
- Jesus did good things and served others everywhere He went.
- Have you noticed how often Jesus uses questions to challenge people to get them to think? Pay close attention to this going forward. He knows that questions help us accept accountability and take action. They help us move from a listener to a doer.

What would I do?

- Let's assume I have an opportunity to help a disabled woman from my church family move out of her home. Her home is the worst-looking and most foul-smelling disaster I have ever experienced—with bugs in there, too. But I know she really needs help and looks to me as a friend. Will I help?
- When I walk among people in stores, streets, airports, or elsewhere, do I try to follow Jesus's example by noticing and helping people

who need a hand? Am I quick with a friendly word and a smile? Am I a point of light for others?

- Perhaps I have a friend or a child who is making bad decisions—constantly! I see the pattern, and I know where it's headed. I've tried to explain, but it's not getting through. What question(s) can I ask this person that would plant a seed of action? This is a golden nugget technique for influencing people. Ask instead of telling. Plant instead of pushing.

Part Three

The Master Teacher

Love from Above

And [Jacob] dreamed, and behold a ladder set up on the earth, and the top of it reached to heaven.

—Genesis 28:12

When we climb the Ladder of Discipleship, we never have to wonder where it leads. Jesus is not only climbing this ladder along with us, but He is also at the top, cheering us on.[35]

—Rob Ladd

My Upward Climb

As I perceive more of Jesus's greatness and wisdom and fill my heart with belief in Him, do I see the climb more clearly and desire to climb more dearly?

Chapter 10

What Matters Most?

Have you ever paused before you bought a book so you could first find out more about the author? Perhaps you were thinking, "Says who? Is this credible and will it be worth my time?"

What about Jesus? The stories of His miracles had generated sensational curiosity and large crowds; surely these reports increased His credibility in the eyes of most. Very likely, the Lord provided those miracles to mercifully soften hearts and encourage belief.

But you and I know even more. We have the advantage of hindsight. Those who heard Him teach were completely unaware of what you're about to see. In fact, it was not known generally until after His death and resurrection. Let's briefly fast-forward.

Who Is This Master Teacher?

If we nudge our story ahead by about one year, we see Jesus walking into a "high mountain," followed only by Peter, James, and John. During that brief time together, the three apostles experienced something that we should all try to envision and never forget. We read that Jesus was:

> *Transfigured before them: and his face did shine as the sun, and his raiment [clothing] became shining, exceeding white as snow.*
>
> *And, behold, there appeared unto them Moses and Elias talking with him.*
>
> *While he yet spake, behold, a bright cloud overshadowed them: and behold a voice out of the cloud, which said, "This is my beloved Son, in whom I am well pleased; hear ye him."*
>
> *And when the disciples heard it, they fell on their face, and were sore afraid. (Matthew 17:2-3, 5-6, with merged excerpt from Mark 9:3)*

Jesus's face shone *like the sun*. His clothing too was shining, white, and glorious. Can you imagine the awe of that moment? Can you picture it—the same intensity as looking into the sun?

Jesus and the apostles then heard the voice of God the Father, from heaven, declaring that Jesus is His Son. This was undeniable proof—to the fullness of the apostles' senses—that Jesus is the Son of God, the very Messiah. As you will see later, this event was stamped into the apostles' minds for the rest of their lives.

Perhaps glancing at the full sun on a cloudless day can remind us of who that person was, teaching throughout the ancient land of Israel. Should He not receive our most earnest attention?

The Sermon on the Mount

Going back now, about one year before the transfiguration experience, we see Jesus walking up the slope of another hill followed by an immense crowd. He seats Himself near the top, and the masses surround Him on the slope below, facing uphill, settling themselves on tufts of grass and flat rocks, as in a natural amphitheater, waiting for him to begin.

If we had such an opportunity today and we knew who the teacher really was, could any of us in our right mind say, "Nah, I'm not interested. I'm almost up to level 68 in my favorite game," or "I've got laundry to do. I can't make it"? Would we not run to hear what He has to say?

Who Is Really Blessed?

Jesus begins, speaking authoritatively but also with kindly nurture and encouragement. He says:

> *"Blessed are the poor in spirit, for theirs is the kingdom of heaven.*
>
> *"Blessed are they that mourn, for they shall be comforted.*
>
> *"Blessed are the meek, for they shall inherit the earth." (Matthew 5:3-5)*

What? That's the big message? Those are the first things Jesus says? Some in the crowd might be scratching their heads and glancing at each other. "People who are poor, mourning, and meek don't sound very blessed," they might be thinking.

Let's consider it a little more closely, though.

These sayings smash the incorrect belief that the wealthy, the powerful, and the strong—the people who appear to "have it all"—are the blessed ones. Forget it. It's wrong. Jesus will show us how we are truly blessed even when we are poor in spirit, mourning, or meek.

Making Sense of Scripture

What Does It Mean to Be Blessed?

"Blessed" is a common word and not always understood. When we are blessed, we are receiving gifts and grace from God. He wants to bless you with the best things in life. But what are the *best* things? Throughout this entire sermon, Jesus is saying, in effect: You are blessed if you make the growth of your soul and the things of heaven your top priority. Get your head out of the things of this world, because they don't matter. Happiness is not having money, fun, good looks, the most dates, perfect children, medals, honors, or the best job. It's becoming what God our Father intended us to become, which means that the challenges and pains we face along the way are actually blessings to help us.

The Beatitudes

Jesus shared a total of eight ways in which we are truly blessed. These eight sayings are known as *the Beatitudes.*

There's a great deal of wisdom here, but it requires a close look. You'll notice that Jesus starts by describing a person who is a spiritual novice and then develops more advanced, spiritually mature behaviors.

You can think of the Beatitudes as a staircase to developing a godly character.

1. "Blessed are the poor in spirit."

We all start somewhere. When we're spiritually poor and have a healthy recognition of it, we think like this:

"Spiritual things don't make much sense to me. I have bad habits that I know I should stop. I'm about at the end of my rope. I think there's hope for me, but I'm not sure. I really need help."

The Hebrew term translated as "poor" is derived from a word that means "to crouch as a helpless beggar."[36] We are blessed when we recognize our "poorness" and how little we can do on our own. We are blessed when we take even the first step to look to Christ.

2. "Blessed are they that mourn."

Once we recognize our spiritual poorness, we often feel sadness and shame about what we've done and who we've become. So, Jesus provided this important promise:

> *"Blessed are they that mourn, for they shall be comforted." (Matthew 5:4)*

Once we understand that this sinful and troubled world is actually a priceless growth opportunity, we can face ourselves and our God with a positive attitude, thinking like this:

"I'm hurting so bad right now, but I've learned to trust that Father in heaven knows what He's doing. I'm learning to find strength in Christ and change my life. I know the pain will pass, that it's just a temporary fire that purifies my spirit. I'm also not afraid of death anymore because—thanks to Jesus—I can be with my loved ones again."

But it gets better still. Whether we mourn because of our sins or our painful hardships, all can be made right in the end. When we strive to follow Him, everything will eventually make sense, wrongs will be made right, and we will look back with new wisdom at our painful experiences. How ultimately comforting.

3. "Blessed are the meek."

Jesus taught:

> *"Blessed are the meek, for they shall inherit the earth." (Matthew 5:5)*

Meekness is a core, Christ-like attribute, but it seems increasingly rare today. Perhaps you already think like a meek person:

"I see more and more people being rude, vengeful, impatient, and demanding—even toward God. And I don't like all of the fighting and harsh words I see and hear on the internet and TV. Can we not show some patience, kindness, and gentleness toward each other? I want to be an example of humility and civility without being viewed as weak."

The Hebrew word translated as meek does not suggest weakness, but rather (1) the humble recognition of our proper place in the universe before God and (2) the recognition of each other as children of the same God.[37]

Jesus was the perfect example of being meek yet assertive. His strength and boldness reflected His knowledge of His identity and His relationship to the Father. It was not prideful belligerence. Meekness is humble, quiet, righteous strength—not weakness—and important enough to be (3) on Jesus's list of Beatitudes.

4. "Blessed are they which do hunger and thirst after righteousness."

If we sincerely and deeply desire to do what's right, we will achieve our objective. The gaps will be closed. Our weaknesses will be made strong. We will gradually become that righteous person we want to be. This is quite a guarantee, spoken by the mouth of the Lord.

> *"Blessed are they which do hunger and thirst after righteousness: for they shall be filled." (Matthew 5:6)*

But desire alone is a car with no gas. As the saying goes, "Eighty percent of success is just showing up." Wake up early. Go where you're supposed to go. Open those scriptures. Kneel in prayer morning and night. Do those basics, even when you don't feel like it. Keep those righteous desires alive and burning in your heart, and you "shall be filled."

5. "Blessed are the merciful."

Would you agree with a person who thinks like this?

"If I can show a little kindness and pity, even to those who might not deserve it, I believe I'm doing the right thing. Some say I'm letting others take advantage of me, but I think it's better this way."

According to Jesus, such thinking is good:

> *"Blessed are the merciful: for they shall obtain mercy." (Matthew 5:7)*

The Hebrew word for mercy is related to compassion, as we would look on a helpless newborn child.

The Roman soldiers and governors were hard and cruel, despising the idea of mercy. Even these days, we hear a lot about *justice*: "I'll make 'em pay for that," many people say. But if we're merciful, we're willing to get over it when family, friends, or neighbors do something wrong—even if they're repeat offenders.

When we are merciful, God will give us His full measure of mercy as He so deeply desires to do. And we all need that.

6. "Blessed are the pure in heart."

Do you feel this way?

"I'm completely honest with myself and others. I want my thoughts, words, and actions to be the same. I'm trying to love what's right and do good things only. The worst thing anyone could ever say to me is that I'm a hypocrite."

Jesus said:

> *"Blessed are the pure in heart, for they shall see God." (Matthew 5:8)*

So far, we've progressed from being as poor as a helpless beggar to having a single focus and desire to love what God loves. That's progress.

If a ring is made of pure gold, it's one hundred percent gold, nothing else. If we're pure, we're not sitting on a fence. We don't show our parents one face and our friends another. We don't follow God when it's easy and give up when it's hard. We don't have a few favorite sins that we hide from everyone and tell ourselves it doesn't matter. We don't lie to ourselves. Purity is single-minded and whole-souled.

As we become more pure, our ability to "see" God grows. We understand more and more who He is and see Him all around us. And ultimately, we will literally see His face.

7. "Blessed are the peacemakers."

Does this describe you?

"I don't like it when people fight. I think it's awful when friends stop talking to each other and family members feud. I'm usually the one who calms people down and helps them understand each other's point of view."

If that's you, Jesus described you this way:

> *"Blessed are the peacemakers: for they shall be called the children of God." (Matthew 5:9)*

Jesus now extols the blessedness of becoming an influence for good in the world around us. Peacemakers are the opposite of troublemakers. They don't light angry fires. They don't start gossip, and they certainly don't fan the flames. They show restraint and encourage it in others. Because of their love of peace, they bless everyone around them.

We are becoming like Christ when we help make peace in our little worlds, so He calls peacemakers His children.

8. "Blessed are they which are persecuted for righteousness' sake."

Jesus had a lot to say about the souls who are teased, criticized, lied about, or hated for doing what's right:

> *"Blessed are they which are persecuted for righteousness' sake: for theirs is the kingdom of heaven.*
>
> *"Blessed are ye, when men shall revile you, and persecute you, and shall say all manner of evil against you falsely, for my sake.*
>
> *"Rejoice and be exceeding glad: for great is your reward in heaven: for so persecuted they the prophets which were before you." (Matthew 5:10-12)*

It's intimidating when whole groups of people unite to reject you. But it happened to the early Christians. And it's still happening to people of all faiths who speak up and stand for something that is consistent with the light of God, especially devoted followers of Jesus Christ.

In the long run, we can "be exceeding glad, for great is [our] reward in heaven."

Did the People Understand?

The Beatitudes were fantastically new concepts to the people sitting on that mountainside. In fact, His teachings probably went over many heads.

Here is a truth about learning spiritual things: we cannot force it. All we can do is allow it in, and let it take root over time. We can pray and ask God to help us understand. Then we accept what we do understand and put the rest up on a shelf for a while and go on living according to the light that we do comprehend. God will help you retrieve your shelved packets of light when you are ready.

Very likely, Jesus taught these things over and over as He traveled throughout the cities of Israel.

The Beatitudes

The ascent from spiritual weakness to Christlike character.

I'm persecuted for good.

I'm a peacemaker.

I'm pure in heart.

I'm merciful.

I hunger after righteousness.

I'm meek.

I'm mourning.

I'm poor in spirit.

His Life and Mine

What did Jesus do?

- Jesus taught us what matters most so that we can let go of what matters least.
- Jesus inspired hope with positive messages that feed the soul.
- Jesus taught simple, sound doctrine about the true goals of life: to develop godly characteristics and function as we were intended to function, with Him as our perfect example.

What would I do?

- What problems in my life might look a lot smaller if I considered what it really means to be blessed? Do I keep the bigger picture of life in mind instead of believing what the world around me says is important?
- Do my actions align with heaven's priorities? Do I really believe that the teachings of Christ matter most?
- When my family members or friends are feeling discouraged, can I be the first to provide gentle encouragement and sound doctrine? Can I model Jesus's hopeful messages and optimism?
- Who might appreciate discussing this chapter with me (for example, by contrasting what the Lord taught us about meekness and purity with the attitudes and behavior we see all over social media)?

Love from Above

"Everyone who does evil hates the light, and will not come into the light for fear that their deeds will be exposed.

"But whoever lives by the truth comes into the light."

—John 3:20–21, NIV

My Upward Climb

Am I ever reluctant to fully believe in Jesus and "like" His counsel and commandments because of my inappropriate behaviors that I love more?

Chapter 11

What's in It for Me?

Me, me, me. When you and I were two years old, we probably said, "It's mine!" a hundred times as we pulled a toy away from our brother or sister or did the tug-of-war with a parent. I'm sure it felt good, and we were right!

We are born selfish, plain and simple. Most of us have to work hard to stop thinking of ourselves and start caring about the feelings and true happiness of other people. But as we do, we become happier ourselves. How strange and unexpected. When we stop thinking, "What's in it for me?" we actually find what our life is meant to be.

Overcoming Selfishness

Anyone still listening to Jesus on the side of that mountain was about to hear Him explain how we can leave our natural, animal tendencies behind and become more like God. He taught five specific things to help us overcome selfishness, in no particular order, but they are arranged and numbered below to make them more memorable.

1. Manage Your Thoughts and Feelings

> *"Ye have heard that it was said by them of old time: 'Thou shalt not kill; and whosoever shall kill shall be in danger of the judgment':*
>
> *"But I say unto you, That whosoever is angry with his brother without a cause shall be in danger of the judgment." (Matthew 5:21-22)*

If we haven't killed anyone, that's good. But Jesus warns us that even our angry or negative feelings toward others can be harmful to us. And we will be held accountable for them too.

Therefore, step one to becoming less selfish and more loving is to watch for our negative thoughts and feelings toward others, let them go, and learn to be positive. We all feel angry impulses at times; it's how we manage them that matters.

How It Applies to Me

Thoughts and Feelings

The above scripture has been the cause of much frustration for some. What Jesus is teaching may at first seem unfair, since thoughts and feelings seem to come out of nowhere. But we can heighten our awareness and recognize the bad thoughts and feelings for what they are. We can say, "Thinking like this is wrong and it's not God's way." Then we let it go before we build up more negative feelings.

As we strive to think positively, we also let go of our guilty feelings about those negative thoughts. Otherwise, we're on an out-of-control merry-go-round, beating ourselves up while wanting to beat up others.

By the way, if we have been abused, our thoughts and feelings become even more intense and complicated. If we have been severely and constantly mistreated, our emotions can grow full of confusion and rage. They are like hungry dogs in the basement that won't settle down until they are fed or released. Ignoring them or telling ourselves we must be evil because the dogs keep barking is not going to work. Seek professional help in cases like this. It will make a difference. Do not tell yourself you are evil because of negative thoughts and feelings you can't seem to control.

Didn't Jesus teach us to be pure in heart? How can we become purely good, over time, if our hearts are full of jealous or angry thoughts about others? It takes an honest and pure heart to be willing to acknowledge what is happening deep inside our spirits.

We can focus our thoughts on good things instead of spending our effort chasing out bad things. We can fill our basket with good apples so there's no room left for bad apples.

2. Shun Sexual Sin

Jesus continued to raise the bar even higher:

> *"Ye have heard that it was said by them of old time, 'Thou shalt not commit adultery:'*
>
> *"But I say unto you, That whosoever looketh on a woman to lust after her hath committed adultery with her already in his heart." (Matthew 5:27-28)*

Sexual relationships of any kind outside of marriage are not appropriate and will eventually cause unpleasant consequences. Jesus says even imagining or wishing for unrighteous behavior is a problem.

Today, sexual relationships outside of marriage are widely considered "no big deal," even among many who are otherwise striving to follow Jesus or other religions. It's as if "we the people" just decided to scratch it off the list. Young people, older people—doesn't really matter. In the world generally, taking this commandment seriously is very rare indeed.

But that doesn't mean there's not a price to pay. Jesus consistently taught that sexual purity is important. Not once did He act as though it doesn't matter.

How It Applies to Me

Sexual Sin Promotes Selfishness and Dulls Faith

Doing or thinking about sexually inappropriate things—including pornography—is like being dipped in wax.

Imagine someone grabbed you by your heels, hung you upside down, dipped you into melted wax, and pulled you out again to dry. Don't worry, it wasn't hot. Kind of comfortable, actually. Unlike candle wax, imagine this wax is kind of rubbery and you can move around freely.

You don't realize it at first, but this wax covers your spiritual eyes, and it's in your ears. It is harder to see, hear, and understand spiritual things. Your fingers can't feel objects as well as they used to. Your spiritual senses have become dull. You also can't see other people around you very well. You begin to ignore or misread other people's needs and feelings.

You need more stimulation to feel anything. You go for another wax dip and come out with yet another layer that dulls you even more. Gradually you see less, hear less, and feel less, and it takes more and more to make you feel anything at all.

Now imagine Jesus standing in the middle of us as we walk around Him, bumping into the things, not seeing well, ignoring each other. By contrast, His enjoyment of life is perfect and unhindered. Many of us can't see this spiritual wax around ourselves and say His teachings about chastity are nonsense. But He sees us perfectly and wishes He could set us free. He wants us to enjoy life abundantly.

Sexual sin leads to more selfishness and dulls our ability to fully enjoy life, truly love others, and believe in spiritual truth. As David Bednar explained, "Love increases through righteous restraint and decreases through impulsive indulgence."[38]

If this seems like nonsense to you, please don't throw it out. Keep it on a shelf. Think about it. Ask God to understand if it is true. All prophets in all ages have taught the importance of keeping sexual love pure between husband and wife.

3. Make the First Move to Repair Relationships

Jesus continued:

> *"Therefore if thou bring thy gift to the altar, and there rememberest that thy brother hath ought against thee;*
>
> *"Leave there thy gift before the altar, and go thy way; first be reconciled to thy brother, and then come and offer thy gift." (Matthew 5:23-24)*

Bringing a "gift to the altar" means coming to God with sincere effort and a willingness to do His will. Jesus is saying, in effect, "If you're trying to do right by coming to God and you remember that you have a conflict or issue with someone else, go fix that first (be reconciled), and then come back to God with your sincere efforts."

Therefore, step three to becoming less selfish is to repair damaged relationships. Be the first to forgive. Apologize if necessary. Be the first to try to resolve misunderstandings in good faith (even if you're not convinced you can trust the other person). Give your best effort. God does not expect us to be someone's whipping boy or girl, but He does expect us to sincerely try to work things out—even with people we don't like very much right now. Often, we need God's strength to even attempt it.

Maybe you already do nice things for other people. You help feed the homeless. You give rides to your friends and bring dinners to families in need. Those are good things, but Jesus requires us to love *all* other people, not just those we feel like loving.

So far, Jesus has taught us to:

(1) Manage negative thoughts and feelings toward others.

(2) Turn away from sexually inappropriate thoughts and behavior.

(3) Humbly take the first step to resolve issues with others.

How It Applies to Me

Commandments Are Blessings

Every commandment Jesus gave us is designed to make us happier. Here is one of the most beautiful things Jesus ever said: "I am come that they might have life, and that they might have it more abundantly" (John 10:10).

An abundant life means it's full and rich, which is what we receive when we keep God's commandments. On the other hand, the Devil tries to convince us that we are "missing out on all the fun" or "wasting our time" if we live the gospel. He is the master liar.

Make the choice today, if you haven't already. Pick a commandment that you don't already follow and say, "I'm going to follow that one. I'm going to do that one today." Keep doing it for at least two weeks and see how it makes you feel. When you feel better and different, that will be a witness to you. That is the abundant life entering your soul, as Jesus said it would.

4. The Golden Rule

This is perhaps the most famous teaching attributed to Jesus:

> *"Therefore all things whatsoever ye would that men should do to you, do ye even so to them: for this is the law and the prophets."* (Matthew 7:12)

In other words, treat others the way you want to be treated. The whole world knows this is the right thing to do, partly because God inspired the founders of most other religions to teach some version of it as well.

Some of the most visible and important fruits of a truly Christian life are being kind and considerate and serving others' needs. We can start within our own family. Taking time and thought to do something helpful and nice is really the essence of a Christian character.

Ask yourself, today, right now: "What can I do for the people around me that would make them happier, lighten their load, cheer them up, make them laugh, or strengthen their faith? What matters to them?" Then pick something and do it. Write a note. Give a surprise hug. Text a compliment. Thank someone. Donate something. Fix something. You name it. The possibilities are endless. (See also *Random Acts of Kindness* on the internet for some wonderful inspiring ideas.[39])

5. Love My Enemies

This teaching may be the most challenging thing Jesus ever taught. To this day, even the most earnest Christians have to remind themselves of this now and then:

Ye have heard that it hath been said, Thou shalt love thy neighbour, and hate thine enemy.

"But I say unto you, Love your enemies, bless them that curse you, do good to them that hate you, and pray for them which despitefully use you, and persecute you." (Matthew 5:43-44)

Back in Jesus's day, this was a stunner. Even though the law of Moses taught that people should, "love thy neighbor as thyself," they focused more on, "an eye for an eye, and a tooth for a tooth." (See Leviticus 19:18 and Exodus 21:24.) The idea of loving your enemies was a tough doctrine.

I have an invitation for you. In all sincerity, please try this:

Who is the first person that comes to mind as "your enemy"? Can you see him or her? Do you feel that annoyed feeling just thinking about him or her? Let's follow Jesus. Pray to God that that person will have a genuinely good day and be blessed in what matters most in his or her life. (Praying that they get hit by lightning does not count.) May their family be protected, may they succeed in their worthy goals, and try to mean it. If you can make a best effort to do that—just taking a few minutes—you will feel something different and better in your heart. Keep doing it and it can change your life.

How It Applies to Me

The Power of Love—Really!

Here is a most astonishing and beautiful quote from a man who knew a thing or two about love and courage—Martin Luther King:

Now there is a final reason I think that Jesus says, "Love your enemies." It is this: that love has within it a redemptive power. And there is a power there that eventually transforms individuals. Just keep being friendly to that person. Just keep loving them, and they can't stand it too long. Oh, they react in many ways in the beginning. They react with guilt feelings, and sometimes they'll hate you a little more at that transition period, but just keep loving them. And by the power of your love they will break down under the load. That's love, you see. It is redemptive, and this is why Jesus says love. There's something about love that builds up and is creative. There is something about hate that tears down and is destructive. So love your enemies.[40]

The Pure Love of Christ

Love your enemies.

Treat others as you would like to be treated.

Humbly take the first step to resolve issues with others.

Turn away from sexually inappropriate thoughts and behaviors.

Manage negative thoughts and feelings towards others.

Natural, Animal Tendencies

Jesus: The Perfect Example of Love

In the end, you know that Jesus was nailed to a cross.

Before that, of course, He had taught people far and wide to "love your enemies." Do you recall what Jesus said regarding the Roman soldiers while they were holding Him down and pounding nails into His hands and feet? This person who had never hurt a soul and taught only goodness and kindness said:

> *"Father, forgive them; for they know not what they do." (Luke 23:34)*

It's unimaginable, almost, except that He is the God of love.

Let's not be intimidated by how perfect He was. But let's be clear that Jesus lived by every word He taught. "What's in it for me?" was completely replaced by, "What can I do for you?"

Consider this wonderful insight from David Bednar:

> *Character is demonstrated by looking and reaching outward when the natural and instinctive response is to be self-absorbed and turn inward ... The Savior of the world is the perfect example of such a consistent and charitable character ... Throughout His mortal ministry, and especially during the events leading up to and including the atoning sacrifice, the Savior of the world turned outward–when the natural man or woman in any of us would have been self-centered and focused inward.*[41]

Making Sense of Scripture

Perfection: It's Good News

Midway in this sermon, Jesus makes a shockingly uncomfortable statement.

"Be ye therefore perfect, even as your Father which is in Heaven is perfect" (Matthew 5:48).

"Really," many have wondered? Well, yes. It's actually a perfectly reasonable statement—provided some clarification. We typically think of the English word "perfect" as meaning "without any mistakes or defects." But we will do ourselves a great favor by getting that interpretation out of our heads when it comes to understanding the scriptures. The word "perfect" has a much more sensible, comforting meaning than that. Consider this quote from Dennis R. Bratcher:

> *The Hebrew word (tam or tamim) does not carry the meaning of "without flaw" as does the term "perfect" in English. It normally means complete or mature or healthy (for example, Leviticus 22:21). That meaning of* ***mature*** *dominates most use of the equivalent Greek term in the New Testament (telos)... From the biblical perspective, "perfect" describes* ***something that functions as it was intended to function.***[42]

Jesus is not merely teaching a list of dos and don'ts. He is giving us (1) a description of the "complete, healthy" character of God (in other words, "what good really looks like") and (2) how to "function as God intended us to function." What a difference that makes! Jesus wasn't condemning us for our weaknesses. He was helping us more clearly see the purpose of our creation: to become complete, mature, healthy, and more godly. (See Ephesians 2:10; 1 John 2:1-6.)

His Life and Mine

What did Jesus do?

- Jesus taught us how to become less selfish and more holy.
- Jesus showed us what unselfishness looks like through His every action.
- Jesus focused outward, thinking of the needs of others instead of inward and worrying about the challenges, pains, or unfairness that He was experiencing.

What would I do?

- Are my thoughts of "what's in it for me?" gradually or completely being replaced with "what can I do for you?"
- What if I'm reading the scriptures one morning and realize that I was snippy and unkind to a friend? What would I do? Forget the

friend and just keep reading? Or make up my mind to follow what Jesus taught me to do?

- Perhaps I've been viewing pornography, and I realize that I really need to stop. Do the teachings and examples of Jesus inspire me to buckle down and get serious about it? (See the endnote for a terrific resource that can help.[43])
- Have I been sufficiently willing to give up my own interests to spend time with my family members or others in need? Are video games, online reading and posting, sports trivia, hunting, shopping, you-name-it-other-time-consuming hobbies, work that isn't essential, sheer laziness, or anything else the Spirit of God is nudging me about right now getting in the way? Can I reduce my focus on these things to show more love in my life?
- Am I painfully aware of a personal struggle, disability, or disadvantage in my life—to the point that I'm challenged to look outward and serve others? Perhaps I am a shy, introverted person, and I hesitate to interact with others. Or I am physically disabled with little access to transportation. Can I apply the principle of looking outward anyway and serve in ways that are unique to my capabilities and situation?[44]

Love from Above

"If a man love me, he will keep my words: and my Father will love him, and we will come unto him, and make our abode with him.

"He that loveth me not keepeth not my sayings."

—John 14:23–24

My Upward Climb

Do I see (or feel) the face of Jesus in my mind's eye?

Chapter 12

Pebbles to Keep

Imagine now that Jesus invited the people listening to Him on the mountainside to get up off the grass, stand, and stretch. What perfect timing for me to share an amazing story with great relevance. Here we go.

Centuries ago in a mystical place, four friends were traveling to a faraway land. They rode their horses down a winding road to a small stream where they found an ancient-looking man fishing at the point of crossing.

"I tell you boys," he called out to them, "you've come to a wonderful place, like no other. Listen to me. See the pebbles in this creek bed? Grab as many as you can before you cross here and take them with you. As many as you can! Down the road, you'll be glad you did."

The friends looked at each other, snickering, not sure what to think of the old guy. The pebbles looked like pebbles. Nothing special.

"If you say so," said one, not wanting to ignore him. He got off his horse and scooped up a small handful.

"What about your friends? You'll find out, down the road. You'll be glad you kept what you did, but you'll wish you had picked up more." He watched each of them closely.

Something about the old man's warning prompted another friend to get off his horse and pick some up. He filled one pocket, figuring that would be enough, while the other two stayed on their horses and laughed.

Weeks later, the friends were setting up camp in the late afternoon sun, when one of them reached deep into his bag and felt a handful of something. The pebbles from the mystical river? He pulled out the largest one and hollered to his friends.

"It's gold! They're all gold!" he cried as he leaped through the camp. Every one of the pebbles had turned to gold.

The two friends who hadn't even bothered to dismount their horses turned white and then looked at the friend who had filled his pockets. He looked sick, hanging his head. "I threw 'em out," he said. "I thought they were a nuisance."

At that moment, the old man's voice was heard echoing in the trees.

You'll find out, down the road. You'll be glad you kept what you did, but you'll wish you had picked up more.

Pick Them Up and Keep Them

Isn't Jesus teaching on the side of the mountain a lot like handing out spiritual pebbles? How many of His listeners will fill their spiritual pockets? How many will drop them after a short time? Look at the many pebbles already handed to me and to you. Let's read them with belief in our hearts, seeking to deeply internalize them and not just intellectually scan them. Let's stuff them deep into our pockets and keep them there.

The Beatitudes

- *Blessed are the poor in spirit.* I'm blessed when I crouch like a helpless beggar, pleading at the feet of the Lord.
- *Blessed are they that mourn.* I'm blessed even when I am sad because of my sinfulness, shortcomings, and hardships. I have the Lord's promise that I will be comforted.
- *Blessed are the meek.* I'm blessed when I humbly remember my place before God and treat others with dignity and respect because they are my brothers and sisters.
- *Blessed are they which do hunger and thirst after righteousness.* I'm blessed when I want to become more like Jesus, when I love the scriptures, crave more knowledge, and desire to repent and do good.
- *Blessed are the merciful.* I'm blessed when I'm willing to forgive and look kindly on others who have done wrong, even repeatedly, knowing God requires it of me to receive His mercy.
- *Blessed are the pure in heart.* I'm blessed when my thoughts and intentions are morally clean, unmixed, and sincerely positive—with no hypocrisy, hiding, or deception.
- *Blessed are the peacemakers.* I'm blessed when I become an influence for good in the world around me—even if it's just with my small circle of friends and family—and I help everyone get along, not fight, and act like children of God.
- *Blessed are they which are persecuted for righteousness' sake.* I'm blessed even when others treat me unkindly or physically harm me because I believe in, testify of, and follow Jesus Christ. (See Matthew 5:3–12.)

Overcoming selfishness

- *I become less selfish when I learn to manage my angry, negative thoughts* by recognizing these are not of God and I must let them pass; I focus on good things instead.

- *I become less selfish when I live the Lord's law of chastity*, which includes being pure in my thoughts and not allowing inappropriate imaginations or actions to diminish my ability to have faith and love others.
- *I become less selfish when I make it a priority to resolve any issues or hard feelings with others*, including my humble willingness to forgive, accept responsibility, and talk to people I think are difficult to love.
- *I become less selfish when I proactively look for opportunities to serve others*, show kindness, and show empathy for others' feelings and missteps.
- *I become less selfish as I love even my enemies* by praying for them and doing good to them, knowing that God Himself showed us the way, pointing us to His true character.

More Christian Pebbles

In addition to these priceless pebbles above, you can read all of Jesus's teachings from His famous Sermon on the Mount in just three short chapters—Matthew 5, 6, and 7. Here are a few more teachings from that sermon, summarized in simple language as nuggets of gold.

"When you do a charitable deed, do not sound a trumpet before you."

When it comes to giving gifts or doing good things for others, Jesus taught:

> *"When you do a charitable deed, do not sound a trumpet before you as the hypocrites do in the synagogues and in the streets, that they may have glory from men.*
>
> *"Assuredly, I say to you, they have their reward. But when you do a charitable deed, do not let your left hand know what your right hand is doing,*
>
> *"that your charitable deed may be in secret; and your Father who sees in secret will Himself reward you openly." (Matthew 6:2-4, NKJV)*

In other words, don't draw attention to yourself. In fact, don't even pat yourself on the back. Just do good and trust that God sees everything and He will reward you openly.

"In this manner, therefore, pray."

Jesus taught what we call "The Lord's Prayer," which includes calling on heavenly Father, thanking and praising Him, asking for forgiveness while we forgive others, asking for things we need, and asking for deliverance from evil while recognizing God's glory and supreme power over all things. (See Matthew 6:8–13, NKJV.)

"How much more will your Father who is in heaven give good gifts!"

When we wonder if our heavenly Father will really answer our prayers, or when we get stressed out about *how* He might answer those prayers, here is some wonderful, even comical counsel:

> *"Or what man is there among you who, if his son asks for bread, will give him a stone?*
>
> *"Or if he asks for a fish, will he give him a serpent?*
>
> *"If you then, being evil, know how to give good gifts to your children, how much more will your Father who is in heaven give good things to those who ask Him!" (Matthew 7:9-11, NKJV)*

"Seek first the kingdom of God."

Jesus taught us how to prioritize.

> *"But seek first the kingdom of God and His righteousness, and all these things shall be added to you." (Matthew 6:33, NKJV)*

We are commanded to put God's teachings and commandments ahead of our own opinions or ambitions. We are to prioritize cleaning up our lives, serving others, and helping them to come unto Christ. Then the blessings will come, in His time and in His way. And let's remember what constitutes true blessedness.

"Don't worry about tomorrow."

Jesus effectively said, "You have enough challenges today and don't need to be worrying about the challenges and evil you may face tomorrow. Live by faith, focusing on the present moment."

> *"So, don't worry about tomorrow, for tomorrow will bring its own worries. Today's trouble is enough for today." (Matthew 6:34, NLT)*

"Judge not, that you be not judged."

We think we see others clearly, but we don't. We show our own foolishness when we think we can fix other people, criticize them, or feel above them. And watch out, Jesus warns:

You will be judged the same way that you judge others.

> *"For with what judgment you judge, you will be judged; and with the measure you use, it will be measured back to you …*
>
> *"… How can you say to your brother, 'Let me remove the speck from your eye'; and look, a plank is in your own eye?*
>
> *"Hypocrite! First remove the plank from your own eye, and then you will see clearly to remove the speck from your brother's eye." (Matthew 7:2-5, NKJV)*

Suggestions or Commandments?

How strongly did Jesus feel about what He taught in this sermon? Do you think He was just offering suggestions? Let's judge for ourselves as we read the words of the Master:

> *"Enter by the narrow gate; for wide is the gate and broad is the way that leads to destruction, and there are many who go in by it.*
>
> *"Because narrow is the gate and difficult is the way which leads to life, and there are few who find it." (Matthew 7:13-14, NKJV)*

The road that "leads to life" is of course the way of happiness—the Lord's way. And "there are few who find it"? That's a rather sobering warning.

The bottom line is that we can't take Jesus's counsel lightly and expect to live with God in eternity. It's plain and simple, clear as day.

Making Sense of Scripture

Keeping the Commandments

It's easy to feel overwhelmed after hearing all of Jesus's teachings. And if you believe it's all good and important, you may want to do it all tomorrow. That's not going to happen, is it?

To find real peace as we commit to follow Jesus, we need to understand what it means to "keep the commandments." Shortly before His crucifixion, Jesus said, "If you love me, keep my commandments" (John 14:15, NKJV). The word we translate as "keep" means to "hold dear, close to your heart, and value like you would keep a treasure." You wouldn't be careless with your greatest treasure, would you?

When we keep the commandments, we hold them like precious gold nuggets and carry them everywhere we go. We try our best to obey them, and we look to the Lord's grace to help us beyond our own abilities—which He surely does. But we don't always get it right. Our heavenly Father understood that from the beginning, which is why we have a Savior.

The bottom line, then, is to give our best efforts to do as He commands while trusting that Jesus makes up for our large and inevitable shortfall. His grace and the power of the Holy Ghost literally save us, cleanse us, and transform us as we look to Him and seek to obey Him. What a grand and comforting doctrine. Imagine it. The very King of heaven loves, lifts, and ransoms even the "lowest member" of His kingdom. How unlike earthly kings. Regardless of how weak I feel, regardless of how unworthy I feel, I can just trust and try to "function as I was intended to function."

So if you're all stressed about what Jesus is teaching, let it go! Seriously, smile. The word "gospel" literally means "good news." Let's just keep these teachings in our pockets and in our hearts, never letting them go and never thinking of them as anything less than celestial gold.

What Did the People Think?

> *And it came to pass when Jesus had ended these sayings with his disciples, the people were astonished at his doctrine:*
>
> *For he taught them as one having authority from God, and not as the scribes. (Matthew 7:28-29)*

I love that. The people were *astonished*—not only by what He taught but the way He taught it. Jesus taught as if He were in charge—because He was in charge and He continues to be in charge. Many of His listeners could feel that this was no ordinary man.

The Apostles' Testimony

Let's return for a moment to that remarkable story when Peter, James, and John saw Jesus transfigured before their eyes. That experience was so deeply burned into Peter's memory that decades later he wrote the following:

> *For we have not followed cunningly devised fables ... but were eyewitnesses of his majesty.*
>
> *For he received from God the Father honour and glory, when there came such a voice to him from the excellent glory, "This is my beloved Son, in whom I am well pleased."*
>
> *And this voice which came from heaven we heard, when we were with him in the holy mount. (2 Peter 1:16-18)*

The apostles didn't follow clever lies and cooked-up stories, Peter testified. No, they saw and heard the indescribable majesty of the glorified Son of God.

So let's remember who was handing out those pebbles. And let's hold on to them.

You'll find out, down the road. You'll be glad you kept what you did, but you'll wish you had picked up more.

His Life and Mine

What did Jesus do?

- Jesus taught us and showed us how to live the kind of eternal life that our heavenly Father planned for us from the beginning.
- Jesus taught us how to function as we were intended to function. He showed us and taught us what right looks like.

What would I do?

- Do I view my minister or bishop—or perhaps even Jesus Himself—as the old man by the river, encouraging me to pick up rocks that seem stupid and useless? Do my friends, social media, TV, and worldly lifestyles just seem more appealing? Would friends laugh if I picked them up? Have I ever deeply pondered the importance of "picking up those pebbles and keeping them"?
- Am I a "menu Christian," who chooses from a menu of suggestions that Jesus offered us, imagining that each of us can just download and use the spiritual apps that we like best? Or do I embrace the fact that I must accept all of God's commandments and strive to obey them in diligence, wisdom, and order—not running faster than I have strength—knowing that I make progress through believing on Jesus, desiring to be like Him, and making a persistent effort to climb as He climbed?
- If a non-Christian friend asked me, "What did Jesus actually teach?" would I be able to summarize key points from His Sermon on the Mount, as captured in Matthew 5–7?

Love from Above

Simon Peter answered him, "Lord, to whom shall we go? You have the words of eternal life; and we have believed, and have come to know, that you are the Holy One of God."

—John 6:68–69, RSV

My Upward Climb

Am I a follower of Jesus because of my love for Him and His light that has filled me?

Or do I do what is right out of tradition or guilt?

Chapter 13

Save Me!

We now return to the mountainside where Jesus had just finished His teaching, still surrounded by thousands. They had heard much today, enough for one sitting, and He kindly sent the multitude away. Fathers, mothers, little ones, and old folks alike filled the roads in every direction, walking in quiet conversation toward their homes.

Scenes like this took place week after week and month after month as Jesus canvased the land of Israel.

The Twelve Apostles

On a certain day, about a year after He started performing miracles and teaching, Jesus called together twelve men from His crowd of followers including Peter, James, and John. He laid His hands on them, giving them power to teach, baptize, and do miracles. This marks an extremely important transition in the Lord's work—from an informal band of followers to a formal organization and kingdom.

> *Then he called his twelve disciples together and gave them power and authority over all devils and to cure diseases.*
>
> *And he sent them to preach the kingdom of God, and to heal the sick. (Luke 9:1–2)*

This is the beginning of the Lord's preparation of these men to lead the kingdom under His direction, after He is resurrected.

Making Sense of Scripture

The Women Who Followed Jesus

We typically envision Jesus surrounded by His twelve apostles as He traveled about, but that's an incomplete picture. We need to adjust our mental movies to include a sizeable group of highly faithful women who traveled with them also:

> *And it came to pass afterward, that he went throughout every city and village, preaching and shewing the glad tidings of the kingdom of God: and the twelve were with him, and certain women, which had been healed of evil spirits and infirmities, Mary called Magdalene, out of whom went seven devils, and Joanna the wife of Chuza Herod's steward, and Susanna, and many others, which ministered unto him of their substance. (Luke 8:1–3)*

Ancient cultures were very male-centric and tended to underreport the contributions and importance of women. It is likely that women were present in many of the remarkable scenes recorded in the New Testament, but they simply weren't mentioned. We don't know.

What we do know is that Jesus broke with the norms of His day and very noticeably treated women with more respect than was culturally accepted.

The Storm

Sometime after the apostles received power from Christ and at the end of a long day of teaching, the crowd dispersed and Jesus and His apostles walked to the shore of a huge lake known as the Sea of Galilee (eight miles/thirteen kilometers wide). They entered a small ship and headed for the other side. Some of His listeners, still intent on following Jesus, also entered small boats and trailed His ship at a distance. Every day lately, Jesus was surrounded and followed. (See Mark 4:35–36.)

We don't know how many people Jesus healed or talked to privately throughout the day, but very likely, the Master was constantly busy and needing rest, so He quickly fell asleep as the ship glided across the lake, but not for long: watch now as the ship bobs up and down on the waves. The disciples' faces darken as they stare up at the sky.

> *And there arose a great storm of wind, and the waves beat into the ship, so that it was now full.*
>
> *And he was in the hinder part of the ship, asleep on a pillow: and they awake him, and say unto him, "Master, carest thou not that we perish?" (Mark 4:37, 38)*

The situation must be dire because His apostles, many of whom are seasoned fishermen and well acquainted with storms, are utterly panicked. One of them yelled, "Master, master, we perish!" (Luke 8:24). And another, "Lord, save us: we perish!" (Matthew 8:25)

Have they forgotten who He is? In the fear of the moment, are they relying only on their experience with ships and seas?

> *He arose, and rebuked the wind, and said unto the sea, "Peace, be still." And the wind ceased, and there was a great calm.*
>
> *And he said unto them, "Why are ye so fearful? How is it that ye have no faith?" (Mark 4:39-40)*

Think of it. He speaks—no, He *commands* the winds and the waves to settle down, and they do so immediately.

Picture the apostles with drenched robes, now leaning on the sides of the ship, breathless and wiping their faces in relief as the waves get smaller and the wind softens? They look to one another and then glance at this man who stands upright in the ship, looking calmly over the waters.

> *And they feared exceedingly, and said one to another, What manner of man is this, that even the wind and the sea obey him? (Mark 4:41)*

Now there is no wind, only silence. Despite all they have seen before this day, each is deep in their thoughts, amazed anew at this calm being walking near them, perhaps smiling and touching them reassuringly.

How It Applies to Me

The God of the Storms of Life

Seeing Jesus literally command the wind and waves was a body-shaking reminder to the apostles that they were not just following someone with a good heart and good ideas. Jesus had power beyond anything they had imagined.

This story is an important metaphor for our lives today. We are each in a boat, like it or not. And we don't know when or how bad the waters are going to be on any given day. But God can and will—when necessary—calm down situations that are blowing out of control.

I testify that this is true. I have seen it many times. When I think my boat is going under and I plead for His help, something in the situation changes, just enough, and I know it is the hand of God. Rarely does God choose to "make it all go away," as He did for the apostles, but He can and will calm the waters in our lives. And when appropriate in His wisdom, He will completely calm the storm for us.

Along with the apostles, let's remember to cry out, "Jesus, save me!" Ask, and it shall be given. Don't ask, and we're on our own.

The Four Kinds of Soil[45]

Right around the time of the great storm incident, Jesus began teaching the people through little stories, also known as parables. These stories seemed pointless to some listeners, but they are truly priceless.

In the old days, sowers planted seeds by walking up and down paths and throwing seeds around, hoping they would land in good places and sprout. Today, we use machines to make sure the soil is just right, and each seed is comfortably tucked into a cozy bed of dirt, ready to grow. By comparison, the poor sower in this story would have been very frustrated:

> *"Behold, a sower went forth to sow;*
>
> *"And when he sowed, some seeds fell by the way side [on the pathway], and the fowls came and devoured them up:*
>
> *"Some fell upon stony places, where they had not much earth: and forthwith they sprung up, because they had no deepness of earth:*
>
> *"And when the sun was up, they were scorched; and because they had no root, they withered away.*
>
> *"And some fell among thorns; and the thorns sprung up, and choked them:*
>
> *"But other fell into good ground, and brought forth fruit, some an hundredfold, some sixtyfold, some thirtyfold [meaning they produced one hundred times, sixty times or thirty times the original seed].*
>
> *"Who hath ears to hear, let him hear." (Matthew 13:1-9)*

When Jesus first taught this story, even His apostles weren't getting His meaning. They needed a little help getting their "spiritual ears" turned on, so they asked Him what it meant.

Here's the key: This parable teaches us about the different conditions of people's hearts as they respond to the word of God. Each of us would be wise to ask ourselves, "Which kind of listener (or soil) am I?"

People's hearts are like soil. Seeds grow best in soft soil, with no rocks and no weeds. The word of God will take root and produce good fruits if our hearts are like good soil. However, many hearts are not like this, as Jesus explained to His apostles:

> *"Hear ye therefore the parable of the sower.*
>
> *"When any one heareth the word of the kingdom, and understandeth it not, then cometh the wicked one, and catcheth away that which was sown in his heart. This is he which received seed by the way side." (Matthew 13:18-19)*

The "wayside" in this parable means the place where the sower walks. When throwing seeds, some would land on or beside the path. The path was hard and packed. The birds liked it, though, because those seeds were easy pickings. No seed would grow on the path because the birds would come along and eat them all up. What did Jesus say about those wayside seeds? The hard ground is like a person with a hard heart who doesn't understand (and probably isn't trying to understand) the word at all. The Devil snatches up the seed like a nasty little bird. In that case, the seed does nothing for the hearer.

> *"But he that received the seed into stony places, the same is he that heareth the word, and anon [right away] with joy receiveth it;*
>
> *"Yet hath he not root in himself, but dureth [endures] for a while: for when tribulation or persecution ariseth because of the word, by and by he is offended" [meaning he gets upset by something and quits]. (Matthew 13:20-21)*

The person with "stony soil" understands and enjoys the good news of the gospel—for a while. But after a short time, his faith is tested and tough times come. The soil in his heart is shallow, and he allows the seed to die. Another person may be insulted by church friends or critical family members, and he decides to give up. And so the seed that grew nicely at first dies soon after.

> *"He also that received seed among the thorns is he that heareth the word; and the care of this world, and the deceitfulness of riches, choke the word, and he becometh unfruitful." (Matthew 13:22)*

Jesus tells us that the "thorny soil" is like a person who sincerely tries to live the gospel at first. They may have good, deep soil. But their other loves and interests, "the care of this world," are also rooted deeply in this rich soil and become more important, choking the life out of the good seed. This person would have been wise to chop down the thorns—those harmful or distracting pursuits—and pull those deep-rooted weeds first. But he loved the thorns and weeds more than this precious seed and therefore didn't bother weeding—at the price of his eternal soul.

> *"But the seed falling on good soil refers to someone who hears the word and understands it. This is the one who produces a crop, yielding a hundred, sixty or thirty times what was sown." (Matthew 13:23, NIV)*

The "good ground" is a soft heart that is open and thinks about the words of the gospel day and night. And what fruit will it produce? It's the fruit of doing good for others around us and keeping the commandments of God close to our hearts, walking in obedience. Are those not the simple fruits of a Christian life?

The good seed of God can change who we are and what we love most. We become an influence for good. We then plant the seed of Christ in others, multiplying the fruit in God's field.

How It Applies to Me

Taking a Stand

Around this time, Jesus taught His listeners a sobering truth: "He that is not with me, is against me; and he that gathereth not with me scattereth abroad" (Matthew 12:30).

What if some of His listeners said in their hearts, "I admire what Jesus says and does, but I don't really want to follow Him. I'm not ready for that. I'm a little afraid to do that, to be honest. What will others think? I'm comfortable with my life as it is."

But again, to this Jesus said, "He that is not with me, is against me; and he that gathereth not with me scattereth abroad" (Matthew 12:30).

Is it really that black and white?

Jesus said it, not me. By not standing with Jesus, our actions are saying, "It's not important to follow God's anointed, to walk in obedience, and to hold His commandments dear." In so doing, by our examples, we are adding to the confusion in the world and the lack of respect for God and thus scattering His children abroad.

The Prodigal Son

Some months later, Jesus was yet again being criticized by the leaders of the Jews. They wondered why He allowed "sinners" to be in His company, even eating meals with Him.

Jesus answered with perhaps the most beautiful and important of all parables. It is commonly known as "The Parable of the Prodigal Son," but in truth, we might better think of it as "The Parable of the Loving Father." This parable is easy to understand. The word "prodigal" refers to someone who wastes something precious. The son in this story represents each of us. The father represents our heavenly Father. Let's consider this important story from the lips of Jesus, line for line:

"And he said, A certain man had two sons:

"And the younger of them said to his father, 'Father, give me the portion of goods that falleth to me.' And he divided unto them his living [meaning he gave him his inheritance in advance].

"And not many days after the younger son gathered all together, and took his journey into a far country, and there wasted his substance with riotous living.

"And when he had spent all, there arose a mighty famine in that land; and he began to be in want [meaning he lived a wild, partying lifestyle and now found himself in deep trouble. So he had to get a job].

"And he went and joined himself to a citizen of that country; and he sent him into his fields to feed swine.

"And he would fain have filled his belly with the husks that the swine did eat: and no man gave unto him [meaning he was so hungry he wanted to eat the corn husks he was feeding the pigs].

"And when he came to himself, he said, 'How many hired servants of my father's have bread enough and to spare, and I perish with hunger!

"I will arise and go to my father, and will say unto him, Father, I have sinned against heaven, and before thee,

"And am no more worthy to be called thy son: make me as one of thy hired servants.'

"And he arose, and came to his father. But when he was yet a great way off, his father saw him, and had compassion, and ran, and fell on his neck, and kissed him." (Luke 15:11-20)

Here, let us stop and consider this great moment in the story. Consider the father. What was he doing? How is it that even he saw his son "a great way off"? His eyes must have been constantly scanning the road in the distance, looking for his son to return.

And who ran to whom? Did the father stand on the porch, arms crossed, tapping his foot, and saying, "It's about time that stubborn boy came to his senses!"?

No, he did not. At just the sight of his son making the effort, approaching the horizon, he ran to his son:

"And the son said unto him, 'Father, I have sinned against heaven, and in thy sight, and am no more worthy to be called thy son.'

"But the father said to his servants, 'Bring forth the best robe, and put it on him; and put a ring on his hand, and shoes on his feet:

"And bring hither the fatted calf, and kill it; and let us eat, and be merry:

"For this my son was dead, and is alive again; he was lost, and is found. And they began to be merry.'" (Luke 15:21-24)

Could there be a more beautiful story to teach us the true nature of God, our Father, and His Son, Jesus Christ?

And what about the prodigal son? His guilty feelings and misery helped him come to his senses, right? Guilt is to our spirits as pain is to our body; we need it to know when we have injured ourselves. But there is harm in focusing too much on our guilty feelings, kicking ourselves and being fearful of God. The son had the wisdom to return to his father despite his guilty feelings.

What was the greater message of this parable? Was it the son's indulgences and deserved suffering or the father's unending love and willingness to forgive?

Doctrinal Points to Ponder

The Nature of God

Our Father who placed us on this earth loves us beyond our ability to understand. He *runs* to us when we just try. He would pick us up and carry us home if it were good for us, but it isn't. We are here to learn to act wisely for ourselves, to see by our faith rather than sight, and therefore He cannot solve our problems for us. But His help is real. His power to rescue is real. And His love is beyond our comprehension.

His Life and Mine

What did Jesus do?

- Jesus miraculously saved people from *anything*. No ailment or threatening circumstance was beyond His power to save.
- Jesus taught us that He hands out the seeds of truth, but only we can prepare our soil, plant it, and care for it.
- Jesus testified of the unending love and patience of our heavenly Father.

What would I do?

- Am I willing to believe that Jesus literally *wants* to help me?
- Do I believe that Jesus can save me from anything, if it is right in His wisdom to do so? That healing the blind, deaf, and crippled

and saving the hungry, sinking, and hopeless are powerful visual symbols of what He wants to do for me—if I focus on Him and believe?

- Do I realize that people can't focus on their spiritual well-being until they feel physically safe and cared for? Might this be one more reason that Jesus taught us to care for the hungry, homeless, and cold? Is there anyone I know who is being (or was) abused in any way and needs my help to feel safe?
- Am I willing to be the voice that testifies of the endless goodness and love of God? Who do I know that needs to hear this from me?
- If I've said all I can to help someone without pushing too hard and damaging our relationship, can I be like the father of the prodigal son and wait for them with kindness—continuing to be a good example while watching for any evidence of a turnaround?

Love from Above

Come now, and let us reason together, saith the Lord: though your sins be as scarlet, they shall be as white as snow; though they be red like crimson, they shall be as wool.

If ye be willing and obedient, ye shall eat the good of the land.

—Isaiah 1:18–19

My Upward Climb

If I have disappointed myself in the past,
do I feel safer and more hopeful
as I see what God is really like
through the stories of Jesus?

Can I hold on to those loving feelings
and let go of false notions and
fears that God is "out to get me"
or is "mean and punishing"?

Chapter 14

The Fish, the Coin, and the King

This fascinating but often-forgotten story occurs *after* Peter was called to be an apostle and *after* Peter witnessed Jesus's face and clothing glistening as the sun.

Today, we find ourselves outside a house in Capernaum watching Peter as he is confronted by a Jewish official. The official doesn't look particularly friendly, and their exchange lasts but a minute.

> *And when they were come to Capernaum, they that received tribute money [a tax collector] came to Peter, and said, "Doth not your master pay tribute?"*
>
> *He [Peter] saith, "Yes." (Matthew 17:24–25)*

As the man walks away, Peter enters the house to where Jesus is sitting. Jesus looks up at Peter, knowing exactly what just happened. As Peter is about to speak, Jesus motions for him to say nothing. Peter had done something wrong, and he's about to get a lesson from the Master. This is how Matthew tells it:

> *And when he was come into the house, Jesus prevented him, saying, "What thinkest thou, Simon? of whom do the kings of the earth take custom or tribute? of their own children, or of strangers?"*
>
> *Peter saith unto him, "Of strangers." Jesus saith unto him, "Then are the children free." (Matthew 17:25-26)*

Now what on earth does that mean?

The tax collector had asked if the Master would pay the "custom or tribute," which nearly everyone was required to pay. Peter answered the man without asking the Lord first. He told the man, "Yes, Jesus would pay it."

Did Peter answer the man correctly? It seems reasonable enough, doesn't it?

What Were You Thinking, Peter?

Actually, no, it was not reasonable. There is an amazing point to this story. Customs are a type of tax, usually charged to foreigners. Tribute is similar. People who were conquered by foreign kings were usually forced to pay tribute—or be killed.

It turns out that the man talking to Peter was collecting the Jewish temple tax—not some type of Roman tribute. This tax symbolized asking God to forgive one's sins.[46] At the time, rabbis and priests were allowed to skip paying it. It's likely that the tax collector wondered whether the Lord should have to pay it since Jesus was regarded by many as a rabbi. But Peter had said, "Yes, Jesus would pay it."

But what did Jesus mean by the "strangers" and "children"? Throughout the King James Version of the Bible, "strangers" refer to people who are not from Israel. The "children of the kingdom" refer to Israelites, meaning the people who are already citizens. Jesus reminded

Peter that countries take "custom" or "tribute" from *foreigners*, not from their own people.

Son of the King

Now let's see if we can make sense of Jesus's comment to Peter. All of us do sin, which separates us from God and makes us "strangers" to God's kingdom. Jesus was the only one on the whole planet who could truly be called a child of the kingdom of God. He had no sin. And He was the Son of the King Himself! Furthermore, the temple—often referred to as the house of the Lord—is His house. Therefore, if anyone should be free from this temple tax, it should be the sinless owner of the temple and Son of the King.

Peter began to see the foolishness of what he had said and how he had made the Lord appear like a regular man and not the Son of the King. He was an apostle, and he had witnessed countless miraculous things. Peter and the Lord both knew that Peter knew better.

Can you imagine Peter swallowing hard, sitting in silence, realizing how he had just insulted the Lord and given a false impression to a Jewish official?

A Miracle of Forgiveness

Nevertheless, the Lord kindly bails Peter out of his decision and teaches him something at the same time. I like to picture Jesus with His hand lovingly resting on Peter's shoulder, with Peter's head bowed, waiting for the Master's counsel. Jesus directs him:

> *"Notwithstanding, lest we should offend them, go thou to the sea, and cast an hook, and take up the fish that first cometh up; and when thou hast opened his mouth, thou shalt find a piece of money: that take, and give unto them for me and thee." (Matthew 17:27)*

The book of Matthew doesn't tell us that Peter actually caught the fish and found the coin, but there would have been no point in writing this story if he hadn't.

How It Applies to Me

God Enables Forgiveness

Bible scholars tell us that a more correct translation of the phrase "piece of money" is "stater," which happens to be the name of a coin worth the exact amount required for the temple tax on two people,[47] the exact amount Peter needed.

Either the Lord knew in advance that a certain fish had the exact coin in its mouth and that this fish would take Peter's bait or He miraculously placed the coin in the fish's mouth after it took Peter's bait.

Even more, this story is symbolic of God's willingness to forgive and erase our sins through the Atonement of Jesus Christ.

Peter represents all of us who have done something wrong when we know better. Then Jesus (or His servants) teaches us why it is wrong. We then receive one or more directions to follow. After we have obeyed, God fixes the problem in a way that we cannot possibly understand. He makes everything right again—as though it never happened.

Has the Spirit of God nudged you recently, helping you understand that you are sinning or carrying a guilty, ugly burden? It's okay. It happens to all of us. Everything can be made right again as long as we desire to fix it and follow God's directions. It will be like it never happened, just like Peter.

The Wisdom of God

There is still one loose end in this story. First, Jesus mildly chastised Peter, explaining how it wasn't appropriate for Him to pay the tax. Then, He told him to pay the tax through a miracle. Why?

The Lord never used miracles to make Himself rich or to take care of His own needs. Why do it now? Certainly Peter could have raised the money—maybe by catching a few fish and selling them.

Rather, the Lord chose to show Peter again that He is the Lord of the whole earth, that He knows all things and has power over all things in the earth. Therefore, in a way, Jesus did pay the money—but only to get Peter out of a jam and to prevent His enemies from accusing Him. But in a way, He did not pay it. No one earned or provided the money for Him; He didn't earn it Himself and pay. The God of the whole earth, Jesus Christ, demonstrated His power again and reminded Peter that He was King of the whole earth and all creatures in it.[48]

Isn't this an amazing story?

Just a Few Lines

This story shows once again how the Bible text often has just a few short lines that are very rich in meaning.

Most of us need historians and Bible scholars to understand the full context and meaning of the scriptures. But now that we know the full background, the story makes perfect sense, doesn't it?

What a priceless example of Jesus's wisdom and power. I love the scriptures and treasure the things I learn from them. I hope you do, too. How wise it is to read our scriptures daily. We renew our witness that Jesus is the very Son of God. We gain wisdom by seeing His wisdom in action.

His Life and Mine

What did Jesus do?

- Jesus never compromised His status as Messiah. To do so would be to lie and mislead. This may seem like a small detail, but the Lord was careful to teach and correct His followers at all times.
- Jesus cared enough about Peter to help him learn from his mistake and then kindly and forgivingly helped him resolve the problem.

What would I do?

- Perhaps a friend said something that made me look bad; she misrepresented me. I know she didn't mean to harm me, but what she said just wasn't true. And I have a right to define who I am, right? There's a time to set things straight, and there may be a time to let it go. If I talk to her about it, how do I express myself?
- Perhaps I have not always represented the Lord or my faith in a way that is fitting, given the many witnesses He has given me. When faced with challenging questions, can I more confidently represent how I really feel about the Lord and His kingdom?
- If I'm trying to correct my wrongs of the past, do I realize that I cannot succeed on my own? (But with faith in Jesus and "going to the sea and casting a hook," I cannot fail.)

Love from Above

Then Jesus beholding him loved him.

—Mark 10:21

My Upward Climb

Does my belief in Jesus make me want to smile and fill me with love for myself, because I can feel the light of His face continually smiling into my own?

Is this a reality for me or just a nice concept?

Chapter 15

Help of the Helpless

Months have passed, and it's springtime again—nearly the time of the great Passover feast.

Jesus's apostles had been sent away on missions some time ago, and today, we see the last of these apostles returning, eager to share their stories and ask for the Master's advice. But the crowds flocking around Jesus are still huge, making it impossible for them to spend time together.

So Jesus invites His apostles onto a boat, and they head for the other side of the sea.[49] Their trip doesn't go unnoticed, however, and many from the crowd follow them by foot around the shoreline.

An Impossible Situation

The crowds eventually find them—numbering five thousand (*not* including women and children, as was the custom in counting crowds in those days). Jesus compassionately takes the time to give to them all that He has—His teachings, His wisdom, and very likely healing those in need. The details are not recorded in scripture, but we know the day was long, and the thousands surrounding them were surely getting hungry.

> *And when the day was now far spent, his disciples came unto him, and said, "This is a desert place, and now the time is far passed:*
>
> *"Send them away, that they may go into the country round about, and into the villages, and buy themselves bread: for they have nothing to eat."*
>
> *He answered and said unto them, "Give ye them to eat." (Mark 6:35-37)*

By now, the apostles have surely grown used to the Lord challenging their faith and their thinking. But this seems like an impossible direction. "Give ye them to eat?" What can they possibly do for such a crowd?

A Meal Like No Other

Jesus allowed the apostles some time to wrestle with His direction, perhaps eyeing each of them from time to time with a twinkle in His eye, subtly encouraging them to think "outside the box" and have faith. But with evening fast approaching, Jesus asks:

> *"How many loaves have ye? go and see." And when they knew, they say, "Five, and two fishes."*
>
> *And he commanded them to make all sit down by companies upon the green grass.*
>
> *And they sat down in ranks, by hundreds, and by fifties. (Mark 6:38-40)*

A crowd of this size is far greater than the population of most ancient villages, so it takes quite a while for the apostles to organize them and get them seated as Jesus commanded. Most likely, nobody is really sure what is going to happen, including the apostles.

And when he had taken the five loaves and the two fishes, he looked up to heaven, and blessed, and brake the loaves, and gave them to his disciples to set before them; and the two fishes divided he among them all. (Mark 6:41)

The scriptures are silent as to just *how* this miracle is happening. Somewhere between Jesus blessing the original loaves and fishes and Him breaking them up to be handed out to the people, they multiply. It appears that He just keeps breaking, and handing out. Breaking and handing out. Imagine the surprise in the apostles' eyes as they see what is happening.

Many in the crowd begin to perceive a miracle, for how else is so much food being provided? Others are simply glad to have a free meal, ignorant and careless as to where it came from.

And they did all eat, and were filled.

And they took up twelve baskets full of the fragments, and of the fishes.

And they that did eat of the loaves were about five thousand men. (Mark 6:42–44)

Twelve baskets of leftovers? Miracle indeed. The leftovers were far more than the original supply.

Make Him King

Like Moses of old, for whom God provided manna (bread) from heaven six days a week, Jesus showed that He was able to save them from hunger. Surely some in the crowd considered this scripture at that very moment, written by Moses over one thousand years earlier: "The LORD thy God will raise up unto thee a Prophet from the midst of thee, of thy brethren, like unto me; unto him ye shall hearken." (See Deuteronomy 18:15 and John 6:14.)

Not surprisingly, after the meal there is quite a stir within the crowd. In fact, some of them want to force Jesus to become their king. "A man with such supernatural powers is exactly what we need. Imagine what he could do to the Romans," they might have been thinking. This is unacceptable, of course. Whether Jesus perceives the peoples' thoughts or it is reported back to Him, He is not pleased by it.

When Jesus therefore perceived that they would come and take him by force, to make him a king, he departed again into a mountain himself alone. (John 6:15)

The crowds are told to go their way, and even His apostles are told to go to the other side of the sea, while Jesus remains all alone. His apostles might have been confused, leaving Him behind like that, but they obey nevertheless and head for the ship. After they leave, Jesus walks up into the mountain and prays for a good portion of the night. (See Matthew 14:22–23.)

Fear Not

As the apostles make the nighttime crossing, the winds pick up and the voyage becomes frightening. Likely, every soul on the boat is thinking back to the great storm that the Master had calmed on command. If only the Lord were with them now.

But the ship was now in the midst of the sea, tossed with waves: for the wind was contrary.

And in the fourth watch of the night [around 3:00 a.m.] Jesus went unto them, walking on the sea.

And when the disciples saw him walking on the sea, they were troubled, saying, "It is a spirit;" and they cried out for fear. (Matthew 14:24-26)

They are shocked at what they see moving toward them atop the waves. A frightening image, barely seen in the night sky, comes steadily closer, step by step, actually walking up and down the dark, rolling waves, unaffected by the winds. The apostles cry out in fright as he comes closer.

But suddenly, they hear a familiar voice.

"Be of good cheer; it is I; be not afraid." (Matthew 14:27)

They had all heard that saying many times from Jesus. In effect, "cheer up, my friends," the Lord was fond of saying. But is it really Him?

And Peter answered him and said, "Lord, if it be thou, bid me come unto thee on the water."

And he said, "Come." And when Peter was come down out of the ship, he walked on the water, to go to Jesus. (Matthew 14:28-29)

Peter Walks

Relieved that it is the Lord and not a ghost, Peter takes courage. He asks the Lord's permission to walk toward Him. What enthusiasm and faith.

Now the Lord could have said, "No, Peter. You're not ready for that yet, my friend." But He did not say that. He said, "Come."

See Peter as he crawls over the railing of the ship. The waves are serious and threatening but this man is pure grit. Everyone strains to watch under the night sky. Imagine the apostles all leaning over the edge, twenty-two eyeballs fixed on that first foot of Peter's as it moves closer to the surface of the sea.

Like onto a hard dirt path, he steps onto the moving but firm water under his feet. And again. And again. The apostles look at each other, stupefied. Sleep has vanished from their minds in sheer astonishment at what they are witnessing.

The winds still howl as Peter moves toward the Savior. We hear waves crashing against the edge of the boat, causing Peter to jerk his head back toward the ship, and then hesitantly back toward the Master who stands firm, smiling, hand outstretched.

But when he saw the wind boisterous, he was afraid; and beginning to sink, he cried, saying, "Lord, save me."

And immediately Jesus stretched forth his hand, and caught him, and said unto him, "O thou of little faith, wherefore didst thou doubt?"

And when they were come into the ship, the wind ceased.

Then they that were in the ship came and worshipped him, saying, "Of a truth thou art the Son of God." (Matthew 14:30-33)

Can you imagine the apostles as they watch Peter—soaking wet—climbing back into the boat, followed by Jesus entering with ease? Some of them stand back in shock, watching as the humbled, drenched

Peter struggles to his feet while the Savior smiles reassuringly at them all. Perhaps some of them even embrace the Lord and feel His comparatively dry clothing.

As they regain their senses and realize what just happened, the apostles worship Him with the greatest reverence, deeply humbled before Him once again.

How It Applies to Me

We Too Can Walk on Water

While it's easy to think of Peter as the man who lost his nerve and sank embarrassingly in front of the Lord and His fellow apostles, there's a better way to think of this story.

Peter is the only mortal man we know of—ever—to have actually walked on water. When invited to come to the Lord—even though it was unthinkable just five minutes beforehand—he did it. And he succeeded. Peter walked on water.

Symbolically, Peter represents all of us as we face challenges that are scary and seem impossible.

Will we step out of our safe little boats and keep our eye on Jesus as we begin to do something we desire that seems impossible to us? Or will we allow doubt and fear to distract us? Will increasing challenges, like howling winds, cause us to take our eyes off Christ and head back for the ship? Because that's when Peter sank like a rock.

Here is a key: The life of Jesus Christ becomes one hundred times more important to us when we take courage from Him and act because of Him. These are not just intellectually fascinating metaphors. Walking on water is something each of us must do in life, if we are to live without wasting life's opportunities.

What goal does your heart want but your head says, "It could sink me"? What have you tried to accomplish with your best, most sincere determination, but you just keep sinking? Are you waiting on the edge of your boat, watching others step out, wishing you were as brave? It's all good. Step!

Jesus was right there the whole time. Peter was never in danger. How often did Peter probably think back on this night later in his life, determined to ignore the winds and keep looking and believing in Jesus—eyes fixed, walking in confidence—because the Lord was with Him?

Help of the Helpless

One of the most beautiful aspects of these stories—whether hungry in the desert or sinking in the waves—is how Jesus helps those who cannot solve their problems without Him.

This very phrase, "help of the helpless,"[50] captures the essence of His character and His compassion. Anyone starved for forgiveness or sinking under life's burdens is never forgotten or without help from the Master.

His Life and Mine

What did Jesus do?

- Jesus dismissed the flattery, whims, and persuasions of men, despite the potential excitement and glory they might offer.
- Jesus focused purely on the will of His Father, which included being an example of serving, helping, and saving.
- Jesus challenged His apostles with hard things to teach a critical lesson: "With God all things are possible" (Matthew 19:26).

What would I do?

- How do I respond when someone flatters me about my talents, good looks, or possessions? Does it make me want to like them and please them just a little more? Or will I remember that only the honor that comes from God is worth receiving?
- Who do I know that is at the end of their rope, exhausted, out of options, and nearly drowning—spiritually speaking? Since Jesus is no longer here in person, can I be the merciful, compassionate, and willing helper who will lift that person back up? Who haven't I seen at church lately? Who is barely keeping their spirits up at home or at work?
- What righteous desire or problem feels simply impossible to me right now? Can I focus more on looking to Jesus and believing in the name of Christ and not just rely on my own talents and willpower?

Love from Above

For my thoughts are not your thoughts, neither are your ways my ways, saith the Lord.

For as the heavens are higher than the earth, so are my ways higher than your ways, and my thoughts than your thoughts.

—Isaiah 55:8–9

My Upward Climb

Has Jesus become my hero yet?

If not, is there any reason He should not be the first on my list?

Chapter 16

The Bread of Life

As Jesus and the apostles awoke the morning after Jesus and Peter walked on water, thousands of the miracle meal eaters on the other side of the sea also awoke, remembering with a full stomach the endless supply of bread and fish that Jesus had curiously manufactured for them.

It appears that some among that crowd awoke with just one intention: "We need to find Him."

But why? Had they begun to believe on Him as the Messiah? Were they hungry to learn more? Or to eat more? Were some of them still intent on making Him the King of Israel?

Finding that Jesus had disappeared and knowing that His apostles had crossed to the other side of the sea, it appears they shrugged their shoulders and figured He had to have joined them somehow. So a good number of the well-fed crowd boarded ships to find Jesus on the other side, probably a day or two after. (See John 6:24.)

A Firm Rebuke

Perhaps after asking around and wandering for a brief time, the crowd of seekers found Jesus in His oft-visited town of Capernaum. Clueless as to how He made it there before them, some of them pressed Him, asking, "Rabbi, when did You come here?" (See John 6:25, NKJV.)

> *Jesus answered them and said, "Most assuredly, I say to you, you seek Me, not because you saw the signs, but because you ate of the loaves and were filled.*
>
> *"Do not labor for the food which perishes, but for the food which endures to everlasting life, which the Son of Man will give you, because God the Father has set His seal on Him." (John 6:26-27, NKJV)*

We've been with Jesus long enough to recognize when He is chastising people, and this is clearly one of those moments. With His perfect knowledge of the thoughts and hearts of people around Him, He doesn't even answer their question. Instead, He gets right to the point: they have come to Him for another free meal. Bread is necessary for the life of the body, of course, but Jesus discerns that that is their only interest.

How It Applies to Me

Do We Ever Miss the Point?

The people seeking free bread seem foolish to us today, don't they? But the story is here for us to learn. Jesus said in effect, "Don't focus on things that don't last." They loved the free food, but did they really believe in what He was teaching?

In our modern lives, do we enjoy hanging out with friends at church but miss the point of what church is for? Are we more interested in church gossip or spectacular news than in a true change of heart? Are we focusing on our money, our looks, or spending our free time on things that don't last, even though Jesus taught us to focus on everlasting life?

So challenged by the Master, they then ask Him:

> *"What shall we do, that we may work the works of God?"*
>
> *Jesus answered and said to them, "This is the work of God, that you believe in Him whom He sent." (John 6:28-29, NKJV)*

This is a very matter-of-fact statement. In effect, "If you want to do what God wants you to do, then believe in Me, that I am sent from God." The act of believing that Jesus was sent from God *is in itself* the foundational action (work) that Jesus is teaching them to do. (See chapters 22 and 23 for detailed descriptions of how to do this.)

Show Us a Sign

I envision this moment in the story as a bit of a standoff. The seekers sense that they have been reprimanded. They may have bristled at Jesus's accusation that they sought only bread, even if they knew it was true. And now they are being told to believe in Him?

Perhaps after a long pause, one of them speaks for the group:

> *"What sign will You perform then, that we may see it and believe You? What work will You do?*
>
> *"Our fathers ate the manna in the desert; as it is written, 'He gave them bread from heaven to eat.'" (John 6:30-31, NKJV)*

What inconceivable impertinence! The apostles are staring at each other in astonishment. Basically the man is saying, "Moses gave us bread from heaven. What will you do to convince us?"

Despite the miracle meal of just days before, they tempt Jesus to provide yet another sign. Are they baiting Him to do it again like a circus monkey or a tiger jumping through a fiery ring one more time? Is this a childish game of "I dare you" to get Jesus to feed them just to prove His point?

I Am the Bread of Life

Now Jesus lays the axe at the root of the tree. His message is basically, "Are you with me or against me? Do you believe me or not?" We have seen these moments before, and we can brace ourselves as we watch Him face off with His tempters. Imagine His stance. See His demeanor. Hear the authority and godly power in His voice:

> *Then Jesus said unto them … "My Father gives you the true bread from heaven …"*
>
> *"I am the bread of life. He who comes to Me shall never hunger, and he who believes in Me shall never thirst …*
>
> *"For I have come down from heaven, not to do My own will, but the will of Him who sent Me." (John 6:32, 35, 38, NKJV)*

Jesus is not saying He is just a prophet or a teacher with new ideas. No, He is the "true bread from heaven"; and like the woman at the well in Samaria, "he who believes in me shall never thirst." That's a line in the sand. Those are statements the Messiah would make.

> *The Jews then complained about Him, because He said, "I am the bread which came down from heaven."*
>
> *And they said, "Is not this Jesus, the son of Joseph, whose father and mother we know? How is it then that He says, 'I have come down from heaven'?" (John 6:41-42, NKJV)*

Here again the people struggle with the fact that Jesus was born of an earthly mother (and they assume an earthly father as well).

> *"I am the living bread which came down from heaven. If anyone eats of this bread, he will live forever; and the bread that I shall give is My flesh, which I shall give for the life of the world."*
>
> *The Jews therefore quarreled among themselves, saying, "How can this Man give us His flesh to eat?"*
>
> *Then Jesus said to them, "Most assuredly, I say to you, unless you eat the flesh of the Son of Man and drink His blood, you have no life in you. Whoever eats My flesh and drinks My blood has eternal life, and I will raise him up at the last day. (John 6:51-54, NKJV)*

These statements seem outright bizarre, at least to some in the crowd. But let's be clear: the more educated Jews in the crowd would have been very familiar with this type of symbolism, especially of bread representing the law and the truth.[51] They might be voicing this complaint just to create contention and doubt. To us today, this teaching is clear because Christians symbolically eat the flesh and drink the blood of Christ (bread and wine or water) as a witness that we fully accept Him and commit to follow Him. Just as food keeps our bodies alive, Christ keeps our spirits eternally alive to all that is good.

Between Jesus's teachings and the confusing protests of the crowd, this rattling of brains has a major effect:

> *Therefore many of His disciples, when they heard this, said, "This is a hard saying; who can understand it?"*
>
> *When Jesus knew in Himself that His disciples complained about this, He said to them, "Does this offend you?"*
>
> *... From that time many of his disciples went back and walked with him no more. (John 6:60-61, 66, NKJV)*

Apparently, some of the seekers were long-time disciples of Jesus whose hearts were not really tuned to His true calling and purpose. Perhaps following Jesus had been merely exciting or entertaining. Perhaps they were not truly interested in the things of the Spirit.

> *Then Jesus said to the twelve, "Do you also want to go away?"*
>
> *But Simon Peter answered Him, "Lord, to whom shall we go? You have the words of eternal life.*
>
> *"Also we have come to believe and know that You are the Christ, the Son of the living God." (John 6:67-69, NKJV)*

Jesus's question, "Will ye also go away?" was specifically directed to His twelve apostles, His official messengers, not to the larger crowd of disciples. Do you think Jesus challenged them with this question because He didn't know the answer? Or was His question posed for their benefit and growth?

Peter was resolute. It's possible that Peter had never even expressed such a powerful testimony in such direct terms before. But in that moment, his witness was sure. We don't read what was in the minds and hearts of the other apostles. Shortly after this, however, Jesus told them that one of the twelve—Judas Iscariot—would betray Him, which Jesus knew all along.

Doctrinal Points to Ponder

Why Does God Say Hard Things?

Why would Jesus say something that could offend many of His listeners, like inviting them to eat His flesh and drink His blood?

Why did Old Testament prophets write that Christ was to be born in Bethlehem, but then have Him move to Nazareth as a young boy, so that most people in His day thought He was born in Nazareth and therefore could not possibly have been the Messiah?

This list could go on and on. The point is this: it appears that God wants us to look past seeming contradictions or difficult things and look at the more important evidence. Let us be careful not to get hung up on a few small things while overlooking the greater things.

How silly to watch Christ heal the blind but disbelieve Him because He didn't wash His hands the way the leaders of the Jews thought He should.

How sad to eat a meal made from almost nothing, only to later walk away and "follow Him no more" because He said some things that seemed strange and didn't make sense at the moment.

God expects us to recognize the truth and goodness of what He has given us and hold on to it, love it, and realize that we don't have all the facts. Love what we do understand and put the rest up on a shelf until we are ready to understand it also.

Little Children

On another day, in another town, we see a group of parents with "infants" and small children pressing closer to Jesus. His disciples, who appeared to be managing the crowds, apparently thought it would be troublesome for the Master to have to deal with children.

> *Then were there brought unto him little children, that he should put his hands on them, and pray: and the disciples rebuked them.*

But Jesus said, "Suffer [allow] little children, and forbid them not, to come unto me: for of such is the kingdom of heaven."

And he laid his hands on them. (Matthew 19:13-15)

Let's imagine this scene in detail. The faces of the parents suddenly brighten as they hear the Master's kindly word. In effect, He says, "Don't stop them. It's okay. Let them come to me." Perhaps He gestured with arms extended, welcoming and waving them to come through the crowd. It's unfortunate that the scriptures don't comment on Jesus's facial expressions. It's not written how tenderly he might have lifted a curly-haired, wriggling little three-year-old onto His knee or held a tiny infant in His arms, smiling as He spoke. But can we imagine otherwise?

On another occasion, the Lord taught something similar:

At the same time came the disciples unto Jesus, saying, "Who is the greatest in the kingdom of heaven?"

And Jesus called a little child unto him, and set him in the midst of them,

And said, "Verily I say unto you, Except ye be converted, and become as little children, ye shall not enter into the kingdom of heaven.

"Whosoever therefore shall humble himself as this little child, the same is greatest in the kingdom of heaven." (Matthew 18:1-4)

How It Applies to Me

Jesus, the Nurturer and Doting Parent

There's something deeply comforting when we consider that He who is "in charge" of heaven and earth spent all of His time kindly teaching, helping, and healing the simple people of the world.

The "living bread which came down from heaven" (John 6:51) fed everyone, including sweet, helpless children.

All of us have times when the vulnerable, perhaps frightened child in us hungers for help from God—a little kindness, a lift, and a blessing to gain strength to do what feels impossible. In these moments, I like to remember this image: Jesus sitting next to me as

He pulls my shoulder to His. He loves the child in me. I feel secure and understood. He is tender and compassionate to the vulnerable, struggling me. This feeds my emotional soul, my very spirit.

He is both great battle captain and tender friend and parent. The humble, loving God, Himself as a child, teaches me what it means to be a true citizen of heaven.

His Life and Mine

What did Jesus do?

- Jesus found the perfect balance between maintaining love for people and challenging or chastising them. He didn't chastise people because of anger and impatience welling up inside, which He then let loose. He corrected them in love and wisdom.
- Whether giving people bread and fish or handing out gold nuggets of wisdom, Jesus used His talents and fully assumed the responsibility given Him by the Father. He applied all He had to doing His duty.
- Jesus took time to love the simple, humble, and vulnerable people of the world, including children.
- Jesus showed us the meaning of true greatness.

What would I do?

- What if I have a friend or family member who amazes me with their foolish decisions and thinking, even when pearls of wisdom are hanging in front of them? Am I frequently tempted to just "go off on them" to wake them up? If I want to follow Jesus's example, do I really think that's a good idea?
- When I'm trying my utmost to minister to others and don't seem to see success, can I remember that Jesus experienced the same at times? But He didn't pack up and go home. He didn't take it personally. Can I simply keep loving them and trust their souls to God's care and keep serving like Jesus?

- Do I ever feel confused by the advice that I should, "Come, follow Jesus, and walk in His footsteps"? Do I sometimes think, "How can I? I can't make bread and fish multiply. I can't heal people by just saying a word. I can't establish a church"? Well, that's all true. But can I apply the talents I have—great or small—within my small circle of friends and family, with the same spirit of kindness and diligence that Jesus did? Can I be a rock and a light for others by living an honest, clean life and giving church and community service, however small, with the same diligence as Jesus—with all glory to God and the Lamb?
- Am I committed to becoming as a child and abandoning the prideful worldly teachings of what it means to be great?

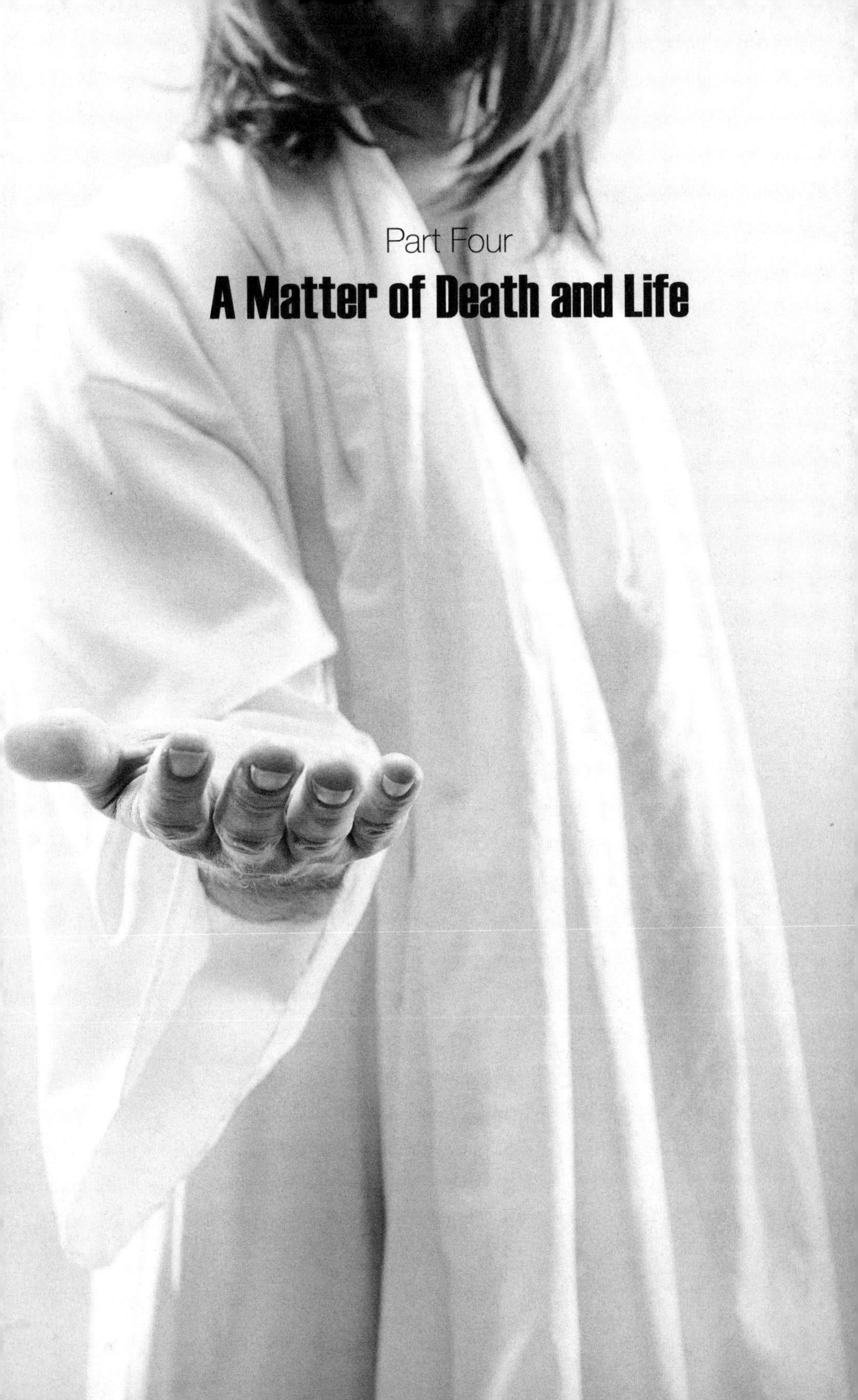

Part Four

A Matter of Death and Life

Love from Above

"Be of good cheer; it is I; be not afraid."

—Matthew 14:27

My Upward Climb

Have I noticed how filling my mind with the stories of Jesus, and believing in them with all my heart, makes it easier to do good things and feel peace instead of fear or confusion?

Chapter 17

Last Trip to Jerusalem

Somewhere around this time, Jesus began preparing His apostles for the fact that He would be crucified and rise again.

And he began to teach them, that the Son of man must suffer many things, and be rejected of the elders, and of the chief priests, and scribes, and be killed, and after three days rise again. (Mark 8:31)

These words seem completely clear to us, but we read that somehow the apostles failed to understand them.

But they understood not this saying, and it was hid from them, that they perceived it not: and they feared to ask him of that saying. (Luke 9:45)

How could such a clear explanation be misunderstood? The *Pulpit Commentary* offers a sensible insight: "The 'saying' was to them so utterly distasteful, perhaps inconceivable. It is possible that they thought this betrayal and death simply veiled for them some bit of teaching to be explained hereafter; it is possible they at once dismissed it from their minds, as men often do painful and mournful forebodings. At all events, they dreaded asking him any questions about this dark future of suffering which he said lay before him."[52]

Lazarus

Nearly three years have passed since Jesus first cleared the temple, "going public" as the Messiah. Now another Passover feast is less than a week away. Jesus and His followers are now on their way toward Jerusalem for the yearly gathering of millions of Jews.

As they approach the town of Bethany just outside of Jerusalem, Jesus learns that a dear friend, Lazarus, is sick and near death. Over the past two years, Jesus had been a guest in the home of Lazarus and his sisters, Mary and Martha, and they had all become very close.

> *His sisters [Mary and Martha] sent unto him, saying, "Lord, behold, he whom thou lovest is sick."*
>
> *When Jesus heard that, he said, "This sickness is not unto death, but for the glory of God, that the Son of God might be glorified thereby." (John 11:3–4)*

The messenger who informed Jesus about Lazarus likely relayed Jesus's words back to Mary and Martha, which their hopeful minds may have interpreted as, "Oh good, he's not going to die."

But as usual, Jesus knows what is happening. Around this time He tells his apostles, "Lazarus is dead" (John 11:14). Yet He chooses to stay right there for another two days.

When Jesus finally arrives in Bethany, Martha—very likely in tears—runs out of the village to meet Jesus and His band of apostles and she falls at His feet:

> *"Lord, if thou hadst been here, my brother had not died.*
>
> *"But I know, that even now, whatsoever thou wilt ask of God, God will give it thee."*

> *Jesus saith unto her, "Thy brother shall rise again …*
>
> *"I am the resurrection, and the life: he that believeth in me, though he were dead, yet shall he live:*
>
> *"And whosoever liveth and believeth in me shall never die. Believest thou this?"*
>
> *She saith unto him, "Yea, Lord: I believe that thou art the Christ, the Son of God, which should come into the world." (John 11:21–27)*

What an expression of faith—just like Peter. But notice again it was the Lord's question that prompted it: "Believest thou this?" Martha already believed who Jesus really was. But His question caused her to look deep into her soul, reach in with both hands, and present to the Master handfuls of her precious faith. And faith is the fertile ground from which all living things emerge.

Around this time, Martha's sister Mary and many who are mourning with her come out to meet Jesus. Crying openly, Mary falls at His feet, with the mourners around her weeping. Jesus is deeply touched and openly weeps with her as well, to which some said, "Behold how he loved him!" (See John 11:31–36.)

We now follow the Master and mourners to the tomb:

> *Jesus therefore again groaning in himself cometh to the grave. It was a cave, and a stone lay upon it.*
>
> *Jesus said, "Take ye away the stone."*
>
> *Martha, the sister of him that was dead, saith unto him, "Lord, by this time he stinketh: for he hath been dead four days." (John 11:38–39)*

Dead four days? No one even imagines that a person dead so long could be brought back. Or do they?

A few men struggle to move the stone that covers the tomb while everyone peers uneasily into the dark, lifeless opening. Imagine the crowd watching silently for quite a long time, perhaps whispering to each other as Jesus, the great Prophet of Nazareth, speaks softly with Martha.

> *Jesus saith unto her, "Said I not unto thee, that, if thou wouldest believe, thou shouldest see the glory of God?"*

> *And when he thus had spoken, he cried with a loud voice, "Lazarus, come forth." (John 11:40, 43)*

After the thundering voice of the Master, there's complete silence. Nobody moves a muscle. All eyes are riveted on the black opening to the tomb which remains as still as death.

Then slowly, a mummy-like figure appears and begins walking out from the darkness, wrapped in burial clothing.

The shocked crowd gasps with one breath, hands over mouths, holding each other, utterly incredulous.

> *And he that was dead came forth, bound hand and foot with graveclothes: and his face was bound about with a napkin. Jesus saith unto them, Loose him, and let him go. (John 11:44)*

Lazarus walks again, awkwardly now because of the mummy-like burial clothes tied to his head and limbs, but dead no more. Lazarus lives again. Jesus restored that which was dead to life again.

Reaction of the People

Words are inadequate as friends weep yet again, hugging Mary and Martha in celebration. How would it feel to watch Lazarus being untied and actually talking and alive? Can you imagine the astonished eyes of the crowd as they begin watching Jesus and follow His every move? Many are overpowered and convinced by this undeniable act of God.

> *Then many of the Jews which came to Mary, and had seen the things which Jesus did, believed on him. (John 11:45)*

Apparently, however, there were skeptics or at least friends of the Pharisees in the crowd. They resisted the evidence, stiff-lipped, like ice cubes that refused to melt in the summer sun.

> *But some of them went their ways to the Pharisees, and told them what things Jesus had done.*
>
> *Then gathered the chief priests and the Pharisees a council, and said, "What do we? for this man doeth many miracles.*

"If we let him thus alone, all men will believe on him: and the Romans shall come and take away both our place and nation." (John 11:46-48)

"This man could displace us altogether," the Pharisees appeared to be thinking. "Miracles or not, He must be eliminated."

Then from that day forth they took counsel together for to put him to death. (John 11:53)

Hypocrites!

Not long after raising Lazarus from the dead, Jesus and the apostles make their way to Jerusalem, to the temple specifically. The great Passover feast is underway, and as usual, the crowds are thick and jostling in every direction. Jesus is surrounded, almost constantly, by both adoring believers and packs of wolves—the scribes and Pharisees—circling Jesus and waiting for the kill.

The wolves ask Jesus questions of every sort, trying to flatter Him, trick Him, and make Him say anything worthy of death. Jesus, of course, knows their thoughts even before the words come out of their mouths. He embarrasses and silences them all, one by one.

Jesus knows this is His last time in the flesh to warn the people about their leaders' examples. We have seen Jesus show great tenderness to all sorts of sinners and forgive all manner of mistakes. But He who fully knows the hearts of all men, and by whose hand all will be judged, thunders His righteous impeachments in a final, blistering rebuke:

"All their works they do for to be seen of men ...

"And love the uppermost rooms at feasts, and the chief seats in the synagogues,

"And greetings in the markets, and to be called of men, Rabbi, Rabbi." (Matthew 23:5-7)

The chief priests and rulers of the Jews love the honor and glory they receive from others. Their hearts are not focused on God, but they crave others fawning over them, as in, "Ah, what great and righteous men we have here."

Jesus continues, laying open their satanic wounds, their infected, oozing sores—right in front of the massive Passover crowd. While pointing to the hillside near the temple, which is covered with white, painted tombs, Jesus condemns them loud enough for the whole crowd to hear.

> *"Woe unto you, scribes and Pharisees, hypocrites! for ye are like unto whited sepulchers [meaning the painted tombs], which indeed appear beautiful outward, but are within full of dead men's bones, and of all uncleanness.*
>
> *"Even so ye also outwardly appear righteous unto men, but within ye are full of hypocrisy and iniquity [sinful deeds].*
>
> *"Woe unto you, scribes and Pharisees, hypocrites! because ye build the tombs of the prophets, and garnish the sepulchres of the righteous [meaning they pretend to honor the dead prophets of centuries ago],*
>
> *"And say, 'If we had been in the days of our fathers, we would not have been partakers with them in the blood of the prophets.'" (Matthew 23:27-30)*

Making Sense of Scripture

Jesus's Rebuke of Hypocrites

At no time do we find the Prince of Peace more cutting than when facing off with hypocrites—those who pretend but do not love truth, those who fight against good but in the name of righteousness, those who claim to honor the prophets, but are plotting to kill Him, the very King of Israel who sent those prophets!

Let's remember, however, that this condemnation was not directed at the Jewish people generally, but at their corrupt leaders. It is simply unfair to criticize the Jewish people as a whole for the rejection of Jesus. A great many Jews believed in Jesus, and a sizable number of believing Christians remained in Jerusalem after His resurrection until its destruction in AD 70.

How many in *our* society today would truly believe in Him and change their lives?

The Loving God of the Old Testament

Now Jesus speaks as the God of the Old Testament, as Jehovah, who loved them since the beginning. He speaks as a parent who tries to protect a dangerously rebellious child. Can there be a more tender description?

> *"Behold, I send unto you prophets, and wise men, and scribes: and some of them ye shall kill and crucify ...*
>
> *"O Jerusalem, Jerusalem, thou that killest the prophets, and stonest them which are sent unto thee, how often would I have gathered thy children together, even as a hen gathereth her chickens under her wings, and ye would not!" (Matthew 23:34, 37)*

Jehovah had loved the people of Jerusalem through the centuries like a devoted mother hen spreads her wings to shield her little ones from fire or foxes, but the little chicks ran off to their destruction.

How It Applies to Me

Metaphors: How Jesus Protects and Helps Us

Jesus wants to keep us safe from harm and help us fulfill our eternal potential. See below the many ways in which Jesus described how He can help us, the little chicks who tend to blindly run off into harm's way.

Throughout his three-year ministry, Jesus made all of the following statements to help us understand that He is our light, our bread, our path, our door, our shepherd, our vine, and our life after death:

> *"I am the light of the world: he that followeth me shall not walk in darkness, but shall have the light of life." (John 8:12)*
>
> *"I am the living bread which came down from heaven." (John 6:51)*
>
> *"I am the way, the truth, and the life: no man cometh unto the Father, but by me." (John 14:6)*
>
> *"I am the door: by me if any man enter in, he shall be saved." (John 10:9)*
>
> *"I am the good shepherd: the good shepherd giveth his life for the sheep." (John 10:11)*

"I am the vine, ye are the branches ... without me ye can do nothing." (John 15:5)

"I am the resurrection, and the life: he that believeth in me, though he were dead, yet shall he live." (John 11:25)

Seen all together, this list is quite a jaw-dropper. What man has the right to say, "I am the person you should look to. I'm it. I'm everything to you. Without me, you are nothing"? No man has the right, only God.

I testify that believing in Jesus with our whole hearts opens us up to His light and power. We are spiritual beings who cannot be saved in the kingdom of God without His light filling us.

The Wicked Have Their Day

The chief priests, scribes, and Pharisees—the hypocrites—chose to disbelieve and plot against Jesus. They might have thought everything would settle back to normal once "the troublemaker" was put to death. But their decision would come with terrible consequences.

Walking with His disciples out of the temple, Jesus said:

"Verily I say unto you, There shall not be left here one stone upon another, that shall not be thrown down" (Matthew 24:2).

Making Sense of Scripture

How Did Things Turn Out?

Jerusalem went to war with the Romans about thirty years after Jesus made that statement. After four years of war, in the year AD 70, Jerusalem was sacked, the temple was set on fire, and the Roman soldiers leveled the temple and most of the buildings in that area so completely that "there was left nothing to make those that came [there] believe it had ever been inhabited."[53] It was unthinkable when Jesus said it, but how true. Most of the temple grounds became like a field, unrecognizable.

Thousands of Jews were crucified at a rate of as many as five hundred people per day, possibly including some of the same young people listening to Jesus and watching Him be crucified about thirty-five years earlier.[54]

How important is it to recognize and trust the word of God?

His Life and Mine

What did Jesus do?

- Jesus "steadfastly set His face to go to Jerusalem," even though He knew what awaited him there. (See Luke 9:51.)
- Jesus exemplified fearless courage by focusing on the joy of doing good, being obedient, and helping others while working through any opposition.
- Jesus raised the dead. Someone who seemed long gone and beyond all hope of returning came back to life.

What would I do?

- Have I considered how utterly fearless the Lord Jesus was in every circumstance? Do I realize how unproductive and harmful it is to be fearful (without beating myself up if I struggle with fear)?
- What circumstance in my life is unpredictable and painful, causing me to inwardly hide? When certain people hurt me, do I respond with fear and then sometimes with anger? Have I taken inspiration from Jesus's example so that I can more consistently "fear not"? Can I imagine Jesus walking fearlessly toward Jerusalem as I follow Him and keep my eyes glued to His back, safely shielded from the haters and tormentors?
- Do I know someone who is nearly spiritually dead? Knowing that the stories of Jesus also have symbolic meaning, can I keep believing in that person—and in God's power to raise her?

Love from Above

I testify that He is utterly incomparable in what He is, what He knows, what He has accomplished, and what He has experienced …

Any assessment of where we stand in relation to Him tells us that we do not stand at all!

We kneel!

—Neal A. Maxwell

My Upward Climb

Do I long to see the loving face of Jesus and sink to my hands and knees in total worship, bathing His feet with my tears?

Chapter 18

The Atonement

Tonight, for the last time, Jesus and His apostles are gathered for a supper. It is the yearly Passover meal, when the people of Israel remember that great night when God freed them from the Egyptian chains of bondage and death.

There is incredibly important symbolism here. Jesus is about to perform the very act that the Passover represented. He is about to deliver Israel and the whole world from spiritual bondage and death.

This moment is a holy one, and tonight, you and I are not invited. It is a group of thirteen—Jesus and the apostles alone. We'll have to rely mostly on the writings of John as we look back on this most important of all nights in the history of the world. As you read, consider that Jesus well knows that this is His very last night with His apostles. Consider that every act and word were of the greatest significance and selected with divine wisdom and intent.

True Humility and Service

After eating a simple supper, Jesus did something that astonished them all.

> *After that he poureth water into a basin, and began to wash the disciples' feet, and to wipe them with the towel wherewith he was girded [meaning wrapped around his waist]. (John 13:5)*

Jesus washing the apostles' feet? Peter actually resisted the Lord at first. He couldn't imagine how it was appropriate for the Son of God to do such a thing. "There is a message in this," Jesus explained:

> *"If I then, your Lord and Master, have washed your feet; ye also ought to wash one another's feet.*
>
> *"For I have given you an example, that ye should do as I have done to you." (John 13:14, 15)*

Could there be any more dramatic show of humility? Doing for others without looking grand? The Master, even the God of heaven and earth, washed the feet of His own servants. Now after washing all twenty-four feet, including Judas Iscariot's, we read:

> *He was troubled in spirit, and testified, and said, "Verily, verily, I say unto you, that one of you shall betray me." (John 13:21)*
>
> *And they were exceeding sorrowful, and began every one of them to say unto him, "Lord, is it I?" (Matthew 26:22)*

How It Applies to Me

Lord, Is It I?

Now here is a remarkable thing. If we put an average group of twelve men and women together in that situation, how many would think, "Is it me?" Or would they think, "I'll bet it's him" or "It has to be *her*"? Consider these insightful words from Dieter Uchtdorf:

"As you hear or read the words of scripture, refrain from thinking about how the words apply to someone else and ask the simple question: 'Lord, is it I?'

"In these simple words, 'Lord, is it I?' lies the beginning of wisdom and the pathway to personal conversion and lasting change. We must put aside our pride, see beyond our vanity, and in humility ask, 'Lord, is it I?'"[55]

Jesus then identified the man who would turn Him over to the Jewish leaders later this same night, Judas Iscariot. He then told him to go and do what he had planned. (See John 13:27.) Judas immediately left.

The Importance of Love and Obedience

With Judas and his evil influence out of the room, Jesus went on to share many of His deepest and most beautiful teachings:

> *"A new commandment I give unto you, That ye love one another; as I have loved you, that ye also love one another.*
>
> *"By this shall all men know that ye are my disciples, if ye have love one to another." (John 13:34-35)*

He had just washed their feet, and He now commanded them to love one another. So important is love; He said that it is the single best way to know if a person is a follower of Christ. That's right—if they have love one to another. Then came another bedrock teaching of Jesus:

> *"If ye love me, keep my commandments." (John 14:15)*

Loving God is the first great commandment, taught Jesus Himself. (See Matthew 22:36–37.) Now, clear as crystal, Jesus told us one way that we show it: by keeping His commandments.

How It Applies to Me

Marriage and God: An Analogy

If you are married or have a boyfriend or girlfriend, you can probably relate to this. Remember a time when the person you love told you something that was important to them? Perhaps it was something they wanted you to do for them? But you didn't pay very close attention.

How did that work out for you? Ha! Probably not a happy ending.

If we ever think that God is so forgiving and so loving that we can do as we please with our lives, we're missing what Jesus taught. Why would He command us to do certain things only to say later, "But you don't really have to do it"? If we love Him, we will remember His words and do our best to follow.

We do not love God or show Him respect unless we keep His commandments. And remember, keeping commandments means we hold them close to our hearts and invest our daily best efforts to obey—just as we would try our very best for the spouse we love, not barely listen or ignore.

The Holy Ghost

Jesus knew He was about to leave planet Earth for a while. The apostles hadn't grasped that yet, but He wanted them to know that they would not be left alone:

> *"But the Comforter, which is the Holy Ghost, whom the Father will send in my name, he shall teach you all things, and bring all things to your remembrance, whatsoever I have said unto you." (John 14:26)*

The Holy Ghost is a member of the Godhead who can actually come into our beings and touch us more deeply than anything else in this life. He helps us remember spiritual things. He helps us know what is true, through deep feelings of peace and enlightenment. What a gift!

"The World"

Jesus spoke a great deal about "the world," which is a term referring to people who base their lives on the trends and traditions that are popular at the time, not on eternal truths. "Worldly people" tend to love things that don't last while equally hating the prophets who teach things of eternity.

> *"If the world hate you, ye know that it hated me before it hated you.*

> *"If ye were of the world, the world would love his own: but because ye are not of the world, but I have chosen you out of the world, therefore the world hateth you." (John 15:18–19)*

Jesus embodies the unchanging truths of eternity. In contrast, the "worldly" children of God are choosing to live without faith, relying only on their shortsighted senses and limited knowledge. When we are worldly, we become prideful, self-centered, and think we know better than God—as many are doing in this Twitter generation. Often, the worldly fight against that which is good as well.

Jesus warned His apostles, in effect: don't expect the world to treat you differently than they treated me. That was an unsettling message, especially considering what they would witness tomorrow.

This Is Eternal Life

As the evening came to a close, Jesus offered a long prayer, mostly asking the Father's blessings on His apostles. At the beginning of this prayer, He said one of the most important things in all of the scriptures:

> *"And this is life eternal, that they might know thee the only true God, and Jesus Christ, whom thou hast sent." (John 17:3)*

Eternal life is our goal and the very purpose for which we were born. It is desirable above anything else. "And the very essence of eternal life," paraphrasing Jesus, "is to know God the Father and Jesus Christ."

How It Applies to Me

To Know Jesus Christ

I was so deeply frustrated years ago that I could not believe in or feel like I loved Jesus. I wanted to, but I couldn't. I had nothing to hold on to. He was just a name to me. But then over time, I learned how to believe in Him, love Him, and actually know Him.

You have likely heard the saying, "It takes one to know one." As we learn more about Jesus, we can live more like Him. As we act and live more like Him, we begin to deeply understand who He is. We begin to feel His suffering and His joys. We begin to truly know the Lord Jesus Christ. And that is when the joy, peace, and light of the gospel become palpable.

Ask yourself: Do you know Jesus Christ better—right now—than you did before you opened the first page of this book? Is the path clearer and the strait and narrow way easier to spot? Is the road of discipleship more real to you now, seeing "where the saints have trod"?[56] Are the Savior's words more meaningful when He said, "Come, follow me"?

If the answers are "yes" and "I think so," then pause and celebrate. That's a foretaste of endless life and a token of things to come for you—eternal joy, peace, and light.

The Garden of Gethsemane

So far, Satan had been losing the war against Jesus. But the fierceness of his hate was just beginning. This night was the moment when the eternal lives of all the billions of God's children hung over the edge of a cliff—all relying on this one person. If He could get Jesus to turn away or to sin, it'd be over.

After what we call the last supper, Jesus took Peter, James, and John with Him to a familiar place:

> *Then cometh Jesus with them unto a place called Gethsemane, and saith unto the disciples, "Sit ye here, while I go and pray yonder."*
>
> *Then saith he unto them, "My soul is exceeding sorrowful, even unto death." (Matthew 26:36, 38)*

Here was God the Son, creator of earth and skies, sorrowful unto death. He had known this moment was coming all along. He knew the crucifixion was coming tomorrow, but His work tonight would be of even greater significance:

> *And he went a little further, and fell on his face, and prayed, saying, "O my Father, if it be possible, let this cup pass from me: nevertheless not as I will, but as thou wilt." (Matthew 26:39)*

The Father did not remove the bitter cup. Jesus submitted to the wisdom of the Father, knowing there was no other way for mankind to be saved. Luke was the only one who described His pain on this night, which was beyond our understanding:

> *Then an angel appeared to Him from heaven, strengthening Him.*
>
> *And being in agony, He prayed more earnestly. Then His sweat became like great drops of blood falling down to the ground. (Luke 22:43-44)*

Too often we think of Jesus being crucified as His great sacrifice. It was but a part. The bleeding from every pore described here was real. It was the crushing weight of that awful burden of sin and guilt for all mankind, placed upon the beloved, innocent Son of God.

Doctrinal Points to Ponder

What Does Atonement Mean?

The Atonement of Jesus Christ enables us to become "at one" with God again. The great sacrifice of Christ brings things together that were broken apart. It can help to think of the word *atonement* as meaning, "at-one-ment."

When spiritual laws are broken, there is a very real price to pay. That may seem odd, but it is true. When we lie, there's a price. If we indulge in pornography, there's a price. We gradually break ourselves apart from that God who gave us life, and that hurts. Our personal spiritual debt totals billions of dollars, figuratively speaking, and we are utterly incapable of paying it ourselves.

To a very small degree, we feel the pain of sin in this life. But in the next life, the suffering will be intense if we do not genuinely accept Christ. Jesus took on those pains—the results of sin—so that we would not have to suffer if we would simply believe in Him and do our best to follow Him. Is it any wonder that believers tearfully praise God for the forgiveness and grace of His Atonement—a multibillion dollar gift freely given?

We may ask, "Do the blessed effects of the Atonement apply to everyone, even me, even if I think I am the absolute vilest of human beings?" Consider this comforting explanation:

> *"The Atonement is unlimited in scope, available for all. The love of God displayed in Christ ... reached out to the whole world, and when God gave His only begotten Son, it was 'that whosoever believeth in Him should not perish, but have everlasting life' (John 3:16). God's desire is to save all men."*[57]

That's right, all men and women. You too. "This is good and acceptable in the sight of God our saviour; Who will have all men to be saved, and to come unto the knowledge of the truth" (1 Timothy 2:3–4).

It is through the Atonement of Christ that we can be washed free of sin in this life, change our hearts and our behavior, and find ourselves fully clean in the presence of God, to be one with Him in eternity. That is what the Atonement of Jesus Christ means for you and me.

His Life and Mine

What did Jesus do?

- Jesus taught important truths, prepared His apostles, and washed their feet as an example of humility.
- Jesus did unimaginably hard things out of obedience to the Father and love for us.
- Jesus trusted the wisdom of His Father above His own.

What would I do?

- When I think nobody understands my temptations, habits, and guilty feelings, will I remember that Jesus did, in fact, experience all of the guilt and temptation that I have felt?
- When life is feeling pretty hard or overwhelming, will I continue to give service with devotion, like Jesus? Can I also focus on the joy of doing good instead of the pains of my afflictions?
- When life feels one thousand percent more difficult than I ever imagined it would be, will I take courage, knowing that even the

Son of God winced at the thought of what He was going to endure, but He went ahead anyway, trusting that the Father knows what is best?

- When someone I love causes me pain, can I take courage from the example of the Savior, who was willing to step up and endure the weight of my foolishness? Can I focus on my love for the person rather than the pains they are causing me? (Remember: being abused is an altogether different matter. God does not expect you to submit to abuse.)

A Hymn of Praise

Beneath his hand, at his command,
The shining planets move;
To all below they daily show
His wisdom and his love.

The little flow'r that lasts an hour,
The sparrow in its fall,
They, too, shall share his tender care;
He made and loves them all.

—"In Hymns of Praise," lyrics by Ada Blenkhorn

My Upward Climb

Do I frequently—even daily—draw strength from my active belief in Jesus Christ and His freely offered grace?

Or do I struggle through the hardships of life on my own, trying my best to think good thoughts, be a good person, and do what's right by my own force of will?

Do I realize that failing to truly look at Jesus in faith every day—even if I'm prayerful and sincere—is like finding a pot of gold and then walking away, leaving it behind?

Chapter 19

I Have Overcome the World

Still in the garden, Jesus breathes, recovering from the agonies and exhaustion of the sins of the whole world. How long he endured it, we do not know. Jesus had obeyed His Father and remained sinless despite every hateful, satanic effort to bring Him down.

The victorious Jesus eventually rises to His feet and walks back to wake up Peter, James, and John, who have fallen asleep:

> *And while he yet spake [to Peter, James and John], behold a multitude, and he that was called Judas, one of the twelve, went before them, and drew near unto Jesus to kiss him.*
>
> *But Jesus said unto him, "Judas, betrayest thou the Son of man with a kiss?" (Luke 22:47–48)*

It's no surprise to the Lord when Judas appears, leading a group of armed guards to take Jesus. The guards are not Romans. No, they are the Jewish guard sent at the command of the chief priests, carrying swords and sticks against the Prince of Peace, to capture Him and thrust Him in front of the Jewish leaders for questioning.

The Trials

After all Jesus had endured in the garden, the rest of that night into the early morning are spent in so-called trials and hearings, all of which are completely illegal. Nothing like this is supposed to be done during the night, let alone during Passover. They rush it all, hoping they can shove Jesus in front of the Roman governor in the morning and have Him dispatched.

First, Jesus is questioned, beaten, and spit upon by the Jewish rulers. When straightly asked, He proclaims that He is, in fact, Christ, the Son of God, stating unambiguously,

> *"Hereafter shall ye see the Son of man sitting on the right hand of power, and coming in the clouds of heaven." (Matthew 26:64)*

He knows such a saying is punishable by death in Jewish law. But His time has come, and He is forthright. Everything has led up to this moment.

After all that Jesus taught and all of the miracles performed, these scholars of the scriptures and leaders of the Jews rejected His testimony and seized on Him.

How It Applies to Me

Peter—A Lot Like Us

During this night of so-called trials, Peter followed close behind, trying to see where they were taking Jesus, listening in when he could. For us today, this could be like following public enemy number one in and around the Pentagon of the United States military. He shouldn't be there and could end up in danger, especially if He were recognized as a supporter of this "false prophet."

At one point, Peter is spotted and pointed out as a follower of Jesus. He denies it out of fear. It happens a second time, and then a third; and he denies each time, even cursing for dramatic emphasis.

During the last supper, the Lord had told Peter he would deny Him before the rooster crowed. Immediately after he denied Jesus the third time, a rooster crowed, causing Peter to realize with horror what he had done, and he "wept bitterly." (See Matthew 26:75.)

Like Peter, we may know things to be true and wonderful one day, but then we lose focus. We may fear and deny our faith. We then feel ashamed. Let's learn from Peter and not give in to fear when the pressure is on. But let's also remember that Peter recovered from the incident. God loves us even when we forget Him. Like the prodigal son returning to the loving Father, He watches for us "a long way" off and rushes to meet us, welcome us, and celebrate our coming to our true selves.

"Crucify Him!"

Now feeling completely justified in their malicious intent, the jubilant chief priests bring Jesus to Pontius Pilate, the Roman governor, saying:

> *"We found this fellow perverting the nation, and forbidding to pay taxes to Caesar, saying that He Himself is Christ, a King." (Luke 23:2, NKJV)*

Mr. Pilate could care less about Jewish traditions and why the Jews would want to put Jesus to death. But he does pay attention when they accuse Jesus of causing trouble in the nation and calling Himself a king. This triggers an episode of political hot potato, running Jesus back and forth between another Roman governor named Herod and more leaders of the Jews. At length Jesus is returned to Pilate, who just wants to settle the whole "Jesus situation."

Now imagine an outdoor stage or amphitheater with a jam-packed crowd, since it is the feast of the Passover. Pilate walks out with Jesus right behind him. Both of them turn and stand, facing the people. Pilate doesn't believe Jesus is worthy of any punishment, let alone death, so he brings Jesus out in hopes of releasing Him:

> *[Pilate] said unto them, "Ye have brought this man unto me, as one that perverteth the people: and, behold, I, having examined him before you, have found no fault in this man …"*
>
> *And they cried out all at once, saying, "Away with this man." (Luke 23:14, 18)*

Reluctantly, Pilate sends Jesus to be scourged, meaning beaten with a whip full of sharp pieces of bone and metal that tear off chunks of skin and inflict deep gashes all over Jesus's body. Pilate stops it at one point, but not before the soldiers torture Jesus more by crushing a crown of thorns down onto His head, placing Him in a purple robe, and mocking Him, saying, "Hail, King of the Jews" (Matthew 27:29).

According to John, Pilate brought Jesus *again* before the crowd, perhaps hoping to stir some pity by showing Jesus in this completely horrid and bloody condition, saying in effect, "Isn't this good enough? See what we've already done to Him?" (See John 19:1–5.)

But the frenzied chief priests are crouched for the kill, ready to spring, already seeing blood. This is the moment. It's their chance to put away Jesus for good. They may have had time to gather their supporters and rile up the crowd against Jesus, directing them to out-shout any believers; we don't know the details. (See Matthew 27:20.) For centuries, Bible readers have puzzled over how so many in this crowd could become so intensely hateful.[58]

As Pilate is about to release Jesus, the chief priests themselves start the rant, *"Crucify Him!"* and the crowd goes along, joining in. *"Crucify Him! Crucify Him!"* they shout. (See Luke 23:20–21.) Whatever voices may be crying out to release Jesus and have mercy, they are drowned out by the chief priests and their supporters.

How It Applies to Me

Suffering Because of Others

There is not a person reading this book, not a person born to earth, who will not suffer because of what others do to them.

Do you have someone in your life right now who is making decisions—perhaps over and over again—that hurt you? Do you cringe when you know he or she is going to do it again? Do you want to just shake them and say, "Don't you understand what you're doing to me?" Perhaps you've already begged them, crying, to snap them out of their narrow-minded selfishness!

Can you imagine how Jesus must have felt His whole life? He watched people do evil all around Him every day, knowing He would someday pay the price for all of those evil acts.

If we knew *we* would have to pay for the misdeeds of others, we would probably run around frantically shaking people and saying, "Stop that! Don't you know I'm going to suffer because of you acting that way?"

But Jesus didn't. With perfect understanding of God's plan, knowing man's responsibility to choose for himself, and with deeper love than we can imagine, He was willing to suffer for the bad choices of others. All He could do was teach by word and example and love them through it all.

What a thought. What supreme wisdom. What an example.

Saying the Unthinkable

Hate is flowing full force now. Satan is raging, and this is his hour. The Devil inspires—no, he *drives*—those who follow him whether they realize it or not. For thirty-three years, Jesus had walked the earth with Satan tempting and fighting Him each hour. Let Him get away now?

Seeing Jesus bloody and beaten isn't enough. With compulsive intensity, Satan's blinded, dark-hearted followers condemn the very Son of God to death:

> *And they were instant with loud voices, requiring that he might be crucified. And the voices of them and of the chief priests prevailed. (Luke 23:23)*
>
> *And they cried out the more, saying, "Let him be crucified … His blood be on us, and on our children." (Matthew 27:23, 25)*

What a frightful thing to say. They condemned their own God to death—and their own children too.

> *As Jesus was led away to the hill of crucifixion, there followed him a great company of people, and of women, which also bewailed and lamented him.*
>
> *But Jesus turning unto them said, "Daughters of Jerusalem, weep not for me, but weep for yourselves, and for your children." (Luke 23:27–28)*

Remember, historians tell us that as many as five hundred people per day were crucified while Jerusalem was under attack, about thirty-seven years from that decisive day and those dreadful words. The Roman siege went on for months.[59] They starved the people inside the city and crucified them when they tried to escape. When the walls came down, the Romans were merciless, slaughtering the fleeing men, women, and children. Truly, "His blood be on us, and on our children."

How It Applies to Me

Captivity: Satan's Power Over Us

It is rather trendy these days to laugh at the thought that there's a devil. But he is as real as God. Jesus warned people about the Devil constantly. For example, during the Last Supper, He said to Peter, "Simon, Simon, behold, Satan hath desired to have you, that he may sift you as wheat" (Luke 22:31).

To "sift him as wheat" means the Devil wants to tear him apart forever, to destroy his identity, and to make him unrecognizable and impotent.

When we resist temptation and choose what's right, we are in control. But when we sin, Satan gains power over us, and we gradually lose control. This is a critical thing to recognize, and it is a scriptural fact. He actually gains control over us.

Sin is like a cancer; it can grow, and we become victims to it. Why else did Jesus say, "Whosoever committeth sin is the servant of sin" (John 8:34)?

Satan has already started sifting us as wheat. Whether we sense it or not, none of us has escaped. We're all partially shredded. And, to varying degrees, he controls us.

There are many forms and degrees of addiction. A daily heroin user's addiction is obvious. A periodic pornography user is on the slippery path to a complete shredding. And on his slide downward, he picks up the additional habits of internal deception and hiding from God as he lies to himself that it doesn't matter and it's just entertainment—plus a host of companion corruptions that come courtesy of pornography. Truly, "Whosoever committeth sin is the servant of sin" (John 8:34).

The most comforting message of Christ is that He can put our shredded selves back together again. We can feel different. We can reconnect with our true selves, like we were as children, with our power to do good reinstated. We really can. We don't have to do the same negative things over and over—things that we don't want to do anymore but can't seem to stop.[60]

"I am the way, the truth and the life," Christ taught. (See John 14:6.) Following Him is the way to true freedom and happiness.

Judas Iscariot

Despite being condemned to death, Jesus had thus far overcome the Devil and his followers—"the world." He had overcome the world through faith and obedience, remaining completely sinless.

In contrast, let's not forget about Judas Iscariot, who was the complete opposite—being overcome by Satan and the world. Judas was literally being controlled by Satan. After betraying the Lord and later seeing what had happened to Him, the final shard of his true self was struck with horror. With the fear of God simmering inside him, he went back to the Jewish leaders, trying to return his reward money. They scoffed at him, saying in effect, "That's your problem," and they turned their backs on him.

Terrified and berserk, Judas threw the money into the temple and immediately went out and hung himself. The Devil achieved the ultimate victory over Judas.

His Life and Mine

What did Jesus do?

- Jesus endured the irony of appearing weak and defeated even though He was achieving the greatest triumph in eternity.
- Jesus endured lies, pain, and humiliation in silence, knowing that He did not need the sympathy of people and that His Father understood His situation and honored His decisions.
- Jesus's focus on obedience to His Father and the preeminence of the things of eternity drove His every thought and act.

What would I do?

- What I am enduring today that makes me look weak or ineffective in others' eyes—and I wish they could just understand my whole situation? Does Jesus's example inspire me, knowing that sometimes only God can fully understand my situation and I must be strong before Him only?
- If I am aware of sinful habits that are beginning to control me, can I draw inspiration from the fact that Jesus completed the Atonement specifically to help me turn from those habits and become free, even as He is free?
- What worldly behaviors are creeping into my life? Are online gaming, social media, and other degrading or time-wasting habits draining me? Are contentious conversations, online rants, or lustful, selfish pastimes overcoming *me*—instead of me relying on Jesus to help me overcome the world?

Love from Above

I am crucified with Christ: nevertheless I live; yet not I, but Christ liveth in me: and the life which I now live in the flesh I live by the faith of the Son of God, who loved me, and gave himself for me.

—Galatians 2:20

My Upward Climb

Am I willing to let my worldly self go?

Am I willing to climb in faith instead of logic and effort alone?

Am I allowing Jesus to love me, fill me, and lift me?

Chapter 20

It Is Finished

The most free and powerful being on earth now continues to submit Himself to the will of the Father.

The work of Christ's Atonement now continues as Jesus is commanded to carry His own cross, or at least part of it, up the hill, where He is laid down across it. There are enough movies that portray the Roman soldiers with hammers and cruel spikes. There is no need to dwell on the monstrous scene.

Jesus is lifted up for the world to see, saying in effect, "Here I am. I did all of this for you. Look to me. Believe in me." The God of heaven and earth is hung on the cross, with a sign above Him that read, "This is Jesus, the King of the Jews." (See Matthew 27:37.)

Still blind and inspired by Satan, the chief priests, Roman soldiers, and Jewish passers-by make sickening remarks as He hangs there:

> *"If thou be the Son of God, come down from the cross."*

Likewise also the chief priests mocking him, with the scribes and elders, said,

"He saved others; himself he cannot save. If he be the King of Israel, let him now come down from the cross, and we will believe him." (Matthew 27:40-42)

Watching Jesus suffer was a great triumph to the chief priests. Or did they possibly have foreboding fears stuffed down to their feet where they hoped to not feel it?

Now from the sixth hour there was darkness over all the land unto the ninth hour. (Matthew 27:45)

Darkness in the middle of the day? That would be quite distressing if you're guilty of conspiring against the Son of God.

The Final Hours

Jesus hung in agony in the darkness, with some of His closest followers suffering nearby, watching and weeping in support. But did any of them remember He had said:

"Therefore My Father loves Me, because I lay down My life that I may take it again.

"No one takes it from Me, but I lay it down of Myself. I have power to lay it down, and I have power to take it again. This command I have received from My Father." (John 10:17-18, NKJV)

Jesus was not being killed. Nobody took His life. "To this end was I born," He had told Pilate (John 18:37). He who knew the beginning from the end had taught His followers that this moment would come.

How It Applies to Me

It's Not Fair

How often, particularly as children, have we complained, "It's not fair!" Over time, however, we tend to say that less and less.

Why? Because it's true. Over time, we learn that life isn't fair. Life isn't meant to be fair. It's meant to accomplish God's purposes in our lives, which includes growth, sacrifice, and pain. You are walking a path designed just for you.

Was life fair to Jesus—the only sinless person to walk the earth to then pay the price of sin for every one of us who messed up our lives? Was it fair to always teach truth and wisdom, only to be accused of being a deceiver? Was it fair that the very night before He was crucified, He paid the price of all of the sins for those same men who plotted to kill Him, as well as those who pounded nails through His bones?

Was Jesus ever frustrated by it all? He may have felt the tendency, but His perfect mastery of spirit and the knowledge of His great mission surely enabled Him to overcome.

So it can be for you and me, as we grow wiser. Each of us, without question, will endure things that are *ridiculously* unfair, and that's okay. Think of it as an opportunity to learn submission, greater faith in the true purpose of life, and Christlike behavior. Think of it as your personalized training plan for becoming the person God knows you can be.

It Is Finished

Jesus knew the moment when His work was complete. His triumph over Satan was perfect. Jesus won the fight through faith, honesty, humility, service, kindness, love, and His great Atonement for all mankind.

> *And when Jesus had cried with a loud voice, he said, "Father, into thy hands I commend my spirit. It is finished:" and having said thus, he gave up the ghost. (John 19:30, merged into Luke 23:46)*

> *And, behold, the veil of the temple was rent in twain from the top to the bottom; and the earth did quake, and the rocks rent [broke into pieces]. (Matthew 27:51)*

Amazingly, the earth shook at exactly the time that Jesus gave up the ghost.

> *Now when the centurion [a Roman army officer], and they that were with him, watching Jesus, saw the earthquake, and those things that were done, they feared greatly, saying, "Truly this was the Son of God." (Matthew 27:54)*

While the God of heaven and earth suffered, there were hours of darkness, followed by earthquakes. Coincidence? Perhaps to some. But the tearing in two of the veil of the temple? Impossible, except by the hand of God. Read on.

Making Sense of Scripture

The Veil of the Temple

A veil is a cloth that hides or blocks something from view. The Jewish temple in Jerusalem had a veil that prevented anyone from seeing the holiest, innermost part of the temple. This room, called the Holy of Holies, represented the very presence of God.

This veil was at least fifty feet high and, according to early Jewish tradition, incredibly heavy and as thick as a man's hand, although this is possibly an exaggeration.[61] But without question, nobody could just walk in there and slash it with a sword—not a chance. Even a moderate earthquake would not have torn a fabric like that all the way down the middle. When the chief priests discovered that the veil to this holiest of all places in their temple was literally sliced in half, they had to be in complete shock and full of fear.

More importantly, think about the symbolism here: it is powerful. This thick, dark veil kept the people of Israel out of the presence of God. Based on the law of Moses, a priest went through that veil once per year. This priest symbolized Christ, going where none of us could go. When Jesus finished His work, He opened the veil for us to freely come to God—through Him and not through a priest.

The law of Moses was over. Nowhere in all of the Jewish religion would this point be made more powerfully than God Himself splitting the veil to this holiest of all rooms. It is as though Jesus's Spirit left the cross, went over to the temple, and tore it Himself before moving on to the world of spirits.

It was over. The Messiah had come and He had finished His work. (See Hebrews 9 for a complete and beautiful description.)

His Life and Mine

What did Jesus do?

- When people lied, Jesus endured it. When they mocked, He remained silent. When people said foolish things that would later condemn them, He left them to their inevitable consequences.
- When Jesus was persecuted, He did not fight back in anger. He stayed focused and walked in a straight course, doing what was necessary.

What would I do?

- What if my child or friend behaves badly and they are cocky about it as well? Will I remember the great example of the Master, knowing that sometimes it's best to remain silent and entrust their care and discipline to God?
- When strangers, friends, or family members hurt me on purpose or otherwise, will I allow the great example of Christ to give me courage to be positive and not fight back in anger? Can I "walk a straight course" toward God despite the opposition?

Love from Above

"I am the resurrection, and the life: he that believeth in me, though he were dead, yet shall he live."

—John 11:25

My Upward Climb

Have I noticed that my ability to understand spiritual things increases when I focus on, look to, study, pray about, think about, reflect on, talk about, teach others, and love the Lord Jesus Christ first?

Chapter 21

From Death to Life

Before night fell, a Roman soldier stabbed Jesus deeply in His side to make sure He was really dead. No movement. Strangely, only water poured from the wound in the lifeless body.

Typically, a crucified man's body would have been thrown to a criminal's grave; however, a well-connected, wealthy man named Joseph had gained permission from Pilate to have Jesus's body placed in his own tomb, near a garden not far from the place of crucifixion. (See Matthew 27:57–60.)

Even though Jesus's body was now dead, the leaders of the Jews still worried about something He had said.

> *Now the next day, that followed the day of the preparation,*
> *the chief priests and Pharisees came together unto Pilate,*

Saying, "Sir, we remember that that deceiver said, while he was yet alive, After three days I will rise again.

"Command therefore that the sepulchre be made sure until the third day, lest his disciples come by night, and steal him away, and say unto the people, He is risen from the dead." (Matthew 27:62-64)

Clearly, Jesus's predictions of His own death and rising from the dead were well known. "What trickery might his followers try?" they appear to wonder.

Pilate apparently agreed it was wise to block any attempts to steal Jesus's body:

So they went, and made the sepulchre [tomb] sure, sealing the stone, and setting a watch [meaning the Romans cemented the stone in place and put armed guards to watch over it]. (Matthew 27:66)

The Angels

Envision a tomb, set in the side of a hill, where the Master's lifeless body was gently placed after His crucifixion. There's a great, round stone blocking the entry way, which is guarded by two Romans. The Sabbath is now almost over, and so far the night has been quiet. The soldiers are at their post, pacing about and bored. But their boredom suddenly turns to terror:

And behold, there was a great earthquake; for an angel of the Lord descended from heaven, and came and rolled back the stone from the door, and sat on it.

His countenance [face] was like lightning, and his clothing as white as snow.

And the guards shook for fear of him, and became like dead men. (Matthew 28:2-4, NKJV)

Here again, a brilliant, beaming angel appears and rolls the stone away while the ground shakes—right before their eyes. The soldiers fall in fright as if dead. Even the toughest of men turn to jelly at such a sight.

How It Applies to Me

Fear of the Unknown

Even great and wonderful things can be frightening. We all struggle with it. A wonderful boyfriend or girlfriend may get us thinking about marriage. A terrific job opportunity that is sure to be difficult may make us feel inadequate. Should we accept it?

What about feeling God's light in your life, perhaps for the first time? Now what? Do I accept it, love it, and walk toward it? Or, like seeing a brilliant angel out of nowhere, do I fall down or run away?

Great, powerful, and new things can be intimidating at first. But let us not call good evil or evil good. Our old selves may be comfortable, but the frightening, new, good thing can be heaven-sent.

Eventually, the guards rise and flee. The next ones to arrive at the tomb find nobody there. Mary Magdalene and other believing women approach and find the tomb, and it is open. How long did they stare into the emptiness and then look at one another, worried and confused? Or did they remember His promise? These faithful women then receive an amazing, comforting message from two angels sent to comfort them by their caring Father above who knows the tenderness of their broken hearts.

> *Behold, now two men stood by them in shining garments.*
>
> *They said unto them, "Why seek ye the living among the dead? He is not here, but is risen." (Luke 24:4, 5)*

"Jesus told you the truth," the angels tell them, in effect. He has become the first to be resurrected from the dead! What a declaration.

Doubting Thomas

The first time Jesus appeared to the apostles as a group, one of them was missing—Thomas. When the ten apostles finally met with Thomas, they excitedly told him, "We have seen the Lord." Very likely, they told him that the Lord even ate fish right before their eyes (See Luke 24:42.) But Thomas was not having it.

Poor Thomas. He was probably a great man and a devoted apostle. But for centuries, he has been known to the world as doubting Thomas. Here is what Thomas told his fellow apostles:

> *"Except I shall see in his hands the print of the nails, and put my finger into the print of the nails, and thrust my hand into his side, I will not believe." (John 20:25)*

Several days later, the apostles were all gathered, and Jesus suddenly appeared without knocking or opening a door—in the middle of a closed room, right before their eyes. And to whom did Jesus first speak?

> *Then He said to Thomas, "Reach your finger here, and look at My hands; and reach your hand here, and put it into My side. Do not be unbelieving, but believing."*
>
> *And Thomas answered and said unto him, "My Lord and my God!" (John 20:27-28, NKJV)*

How It Applies to Me

"Be Not Faithless, but Believing"

It's easy to think Thomas was just stubborn. But Thomas isn't all that different from you and me, is he?

I've met some people who are born believers. They knew and recognized the truthfulness of the gospel since they were children, and they grew in the truth without ever a serious doubt. But I believe such hearts are exceptions. They're real but exceptional.

For most of us, the Lord's advice to Thomas is what we need to hear. "Thomas, because thou hast seen me, thou hast believed: blessed are they that have not seen, and yet have believed" (John 20:29).

Thomas was privileged to use three of his physical senses to decide whether to believe Jesus had in fact risen from the dead: he saw, he heard, and he touched.

You and me? We don't have the privilege. We'd better make up our minds to believe. If that's hard for you, be sure to read "Chapter 23: What If Believing Is Hard for Me?" As you will see, there are some very logical and compelling reasons to believe.

Jesus Appears unto Many

Here is a summary of Jesus's many appearances after His resurrection, as recorded in the Bible. The timing and precise order of when Jesus appeared to various people matters less than how often He appeared and the way in which He did it. Did you recall that there were this many appearances?

- To Mary Magdalene, near the tomb (Mark 16:9).
- To other women, somewhere between the tomb and Jerusalem (Matthew 28:1–9).
- To two disciples as they walked and talked together for quite a while on the road to Emmaus. Then Jesus vanished right before their eyes (Luke 24:13-40).
- To Peter alone, in or near Jerusalem (Luke 24:34, 1 Corinthians 15:5).
- To all eleven remaining apostles at Jerusalem (Mark 16:14).
- To all eleven apostles at the Sea of Tiberius (John 21:1–24).
- To five hundred brethren at once (1 Corinthians 15:6).
- To James (1 Corinthians 15:7).
- Finally, to all eleven apostles, just before His final journey back to the Father (Matthew 28:16–20).

How It Applies to Me

What About Me? Will I Live Again?

Being with a loved one as they die of natural causes is kind of like watching a family member as they sail away on a ship, growing ever smaller, far into the horizon. The tiny ship eventually disappears, invisible to those left behind. But where did they really go? Did they "fall off the edge," never to be seen again? Thankfully, no.

Our family member's spirit will simply separate from their body which is left behind, like a hand is removed from a glove that remains lifeless on a table. "Then shall the dust [meaning the body] return to the earth as it was: and the spirit shall return unto God who gave it" (Ecclesiastes 12:7). The spirit is very much alive, as many people who have had near-death experiences will testify. We all return home to the world of spirits.

And our bodies? Will they remain in the grave? Absolutely not. This is the great and hopeful news for each of us. "For as in Adam all die, even so in Christ shall all be made alive" (1 Corinthians 15:22).

Thanks to the power of Christ and His resurrection, we will all be physically, literally resurrected, just as He was, receiving a body that will never get old or die again. Although this belief is dwindling today,[62] Christians historically have understood this as one of the greatest and most comforting doctrines of the gospel.[63]

Direction to the Apostles

The great life of Jesus Christ on earth had come to an end. He had completed the great work of the Atonement. He taught the people of Israel in person, and He showed us all how to live by His words and example.

What next?

After His resurrection, Christ the King personally taught and directed His apostles for approximately forty days. Forty days! That's a lot of instruction to receive directly from the undeniably real, resurrected God of heaven and earth. He taught them "the things pertaining to the kingdom of God" (Acts 1:3).

Now it would become the apostles' turn to lead, their turn to teach, and their turn to be the targets of blind violence and lies. They had seen the Master bear it perfectly. Now, with the help of the Holy Spirit—soon to be given to them—they would assume their offices as the chief servants in the kingdom of God on earth.

Earlier, Jesus had told them:

"He who receives you receives Me, and he who receives Me receives Him who sent Me." (Matthew 10:40, NASB)

Christ was not a storyteller, a magician, an entertainer. He was not a "flash in the pan"—a one-time dazzler of a prophet. He was there to establish an organization and a kingdom to enrich our lives on earth and save us spiritually for eternity.

And Jesus came and spake unto them, saying,

"All power is given unto me in heaven and in earth.

"Go ye therefore, and teach all nations, baptizing them in the name of the Father, and of the Son, and of the Holy Ghost:

"Teaching them to observe all things whatsoever I have commanded you: and, lo, I am with you always, even unto the end of the world. Amen." (Matthew 28:18-20)

Jesus Rises Up into the Sky

And after He had said these things, He was lifted up while they were looking on, and a cloud received Him out of their sight.

And as they were gazing intently into the sky while He was going, behold, two men in white clothing stood beside them.

They also said, "Men of Galilee, why do you stand looking into the sky? This Jesus, who has been taken up from you into heaven, will come in just the same way as you have watched Him go into heaven." (Acts 1:9-11, NASB)

Only eleven were privileged to witness this final, grand scene. How many would believe their witness? How many would judge them as fanatics and deceived fools—as many of us are judged today?

The Second Coming of Jesus Christ

The angels that day—as well as prophets and apostles of old—have told us that Jesus will return. The exact time no one knows, but it is not far.

Each of us is invited—even commanded—to receive Him, believe Him, and follow Him. We are to align with Him and not against Him, to be part of the solution and not of part of the problem.

What could honor Him or please Him more than to find us keeping His teachings close to our hearts and walking in His steps?

His Life and Mine

What did Jesus do?

- Jesus resurrected Himself from the dead, enabling all of mankind to also be raised from the dead. (See John 10:18.)
- Jesus was patient and merciful toward the doubting apostle, Thomas, but also firm in directing him to "be not faithless, but believing."
- Jesus commanded His apostles to teach and testify of Him.

What would I do?

- When the fear of death creeps up on me, will I remember with a burning, believing heart that all of us will be raised to life again as a gift to all mankind—because of Jesus?
- Who do I know that would benefit from a discussion about life after death? (Perhaps such fears never cross your mind, but for many people, it is their darkest, innermost terror. Your testimony may be the relief they need.)

- Will I help the apostles in their great mission to encourage people everywhere to believe in Jesus Christ and to doubt no more? Can I be patient with skeptics and testify of the blessings that come from believing on the name of Jesus?
- If I love what I've learned about Christ and experienced in my own life, will I pray with all the energy of heart that God will help me to help others come to Him?

Part Five

My Life

Love from Above

But the Comforter, which is the Holy Ghost, whom the Father will send in my name, he shall teach you all things, and bring all things to your remembrance, whatsoever I have said unto you.

—John 14:26

My Upward Climb

Do I feel differently, better now, compared to when I first started this study of the life of Jesus?

Do I realize that my study of Jesus has deposited millions in pure gold into my spiritual memory banks, which the Holy Ghost can retrieve for me just when I need it?

Chapter 22

The Eye of Faith

Imagine you are John, the apostle who just walked with Jesus for three incredible years. Reflect back on the first time you met Him, when John the Baptist pointed Him out to you on the banks of the River Jordan. Remember the miracle of water and wine at the wedding feast; the healings in front of Peter's house; His walks among the crowds; His teachings (sometimes one-on-one and other times to thousands); the upper room where He washed Peter's feet and your feet; the crowds yelling, "Crucify him!"; the earthquake at His death; the moment when you yourself saw the risen Savior again; and, finally, the day you and your ten fellow apostles stood shoulder to shoulder, watching Him rise into the sky until He disappeared.

John the apostle saw it all. And by reading about Jesus, we can envision it all. But even after seeing so much, we can potentially remain spiritually in the dark. We may still be standing in darkness at the foot of our spiritual climbing walls—even after such amazing experiences.

Witnessing miracles and understanding doctrines intellectually are not the same as climbing our way up the wall of spiritual light. How do we make sure the gospel of Jesus Christ actually delivers the joy, peace, power, and light we all need?

Turning On the Light of Faith

Believing in Jesus is a conscious decision, a choice. *This choice, this action, turns on the switch.* That's it. We must do that in order to believe in the way the scriptures use the phrases, "Believe on the name of Jesus," and "Come, follow me," and many other phrases like them.[64]

For example, we can literally say out loud or in our hearts—and mean it—"I believe in Jesus Christ. I believe Jesus was sent by God as the Messiah and as my Savior. I believe in Jesus," and similar things. We mean it and think it and say it throughout our quiet moments, while we pray and as we drive. It becomes ingrained in us. We can frequently thank Heavenly Father in our prayers for sending His Son and tell Him what we admire about Him and how we appreciate all He has done for us. We must believe *that* deeply in Jesus Christ.

It's black and white. When we believe like this in Jesus Christ, the light from Christ begins to flow into our lives. When we do not believe, it does not flow.

If believing is natural and easy for you, then celebrate and praise your Heavenly Father. Not everyone finds it so.

What Happens When I Receive Spiritual Light?

Here's what happens when we begin climbing our spiritual wall into the bright light of God. Have you noticed these thoughts and desires in your own life?

- I care more about doing what's right than I used to.
- I notice and admire the good, courageous, and decent people around me more than I used to.

- I understand and like the scriptures more lately. There are a lot of dots being connected between my heart and mind.
- I have a clearer sense of my true identity as opposed to who the world has told me I am or what I should be.
- My view of what really matters has changed; my worldview has changed. I see the earth as small and eternity as large and very important.
- I see how small I am compared to the greatness of God; I want to kneel before Him and praise Him for all that He has done; my gratitude knows no bounds.
- I honestly trust that God is smarter than I am. I'm a fool if I try to resist Him.
- I suddenly understand how to deal with a problem that's been tormenting me—because I now see how to do it Jesus's way.
- I figured out what it means to follow Jesus.
- I'm not ashamed to admit that I believe and follow Jesus. I'm definitely willing to take a stand when it's not easy, and I feel good about that.
- I want to teach others about Jesus and His Gospel.
- I want to help people more now. I want to be kinder and more willing to sacrifice. I want to stop getting so angry.
- I have hope that God can save me from my addictions; I see that the stories and miracles of Jesus are symbols of His saving power in my own life.
- The stories of Jesus have inspired me to tackle hard things in my life.
- I see God as my heavenly parent. I know He wants me to obey Him because He's looking out for my well-being. I truly get that.
- I feel God's love more than I used to.
- I want God to be pleased with me.
- I want to do the right things for the right reasons.
- I want to be like Jesus (and not just because I'm supposed to).

All of these feelings and insights are the effects of the light of Jesus Christ awaking and enlivening our spirit.

How many of these statements are true for you—perhaps for the first time ever? Or perhaps you feel them more deeply since immersing yourself in the life and teachings of Jesus? If so, you have activated your believing heart and climbed up to where you've got a whole, new perspective—a view illuminated by the light of the world.

Humph, Not Me

It's possible that you've felt very few or none of these things as you read about Christ. Your purpose may have been to learn the facts about Jesus's life. Your intent was to be cautious and think it through first. I respect you for that. We must be honest with ourselves. You'll want to read the next chapter very carefully as it was written with you in mind.

It's possible to study the entire story of Jesus over and over and never have these enlightened perceptions and experiences. That's because we can't just noodle over knowledge alone and expect to experience the light and living water of Christ. It doesn't work that way. It takes (1) belief, (2) repentance, and (3) following the example of Jesus.

So explained Dieter Uchtdorf: "When we choose to believe, exercise faith unto repentance, and follow our Savior, Jesus Christ, we open our spiritual eyes to splendors we can scarcely imagine. Thus our belief and faith will grow stronger, and we will see even more."[65]

The Faucet Analogy

Jesus also compared His power to "living water." Not just any water. Living water. Water that is itself alive. Water that imbues spiritual life. The concepts of light, water, and life are very similar in scripture.

Christ's living water is like pressurized water. It "wants" to come out. As soon as someone opens the valve (the faucet handle), it will automatically flow.

The faucet handle stops or starts the water flowing. The spiritual actions that stop the water are lack of belief and unwillingness to believe. The action that starts the water is belief in Jesus Christ specifically. (Granted, other forms of belief in God and spiritual truths release some water, but from the perspective of the gospel of Jesus

Christ, belief and the exercise of faith must be centered in Him to truly receive the fullness of living water.)

Most faucets have screens at the opening. Although the living water is always pure and clean, our screens are not. Screens either block the flow of water or allow it to pass. Our spiritual filthiness creates dirty, gunked-up screens. Fortunately, they never completely shut off the water, but they can slow it to mere drops.

We clean the screen by our willingness to change, and then we actually change/repent in partnership with God, as mentioned throughout this book and explained in detail throughout the New Testament.

In summary, the full force of living water that "wants" to come out and bless us is there, waiting for us to (1) fully open the valve through more and more active exercise of faith and (2) continually remove gunk and embrace virtuous principles as we walk in the steps of the Savior, Jesus Christ.

Now look back at those examples of spiritual light listed earlier; they represent the light and the living water God wants to shine and to pour into your life. How many have trickled in for you? How many are flowing so hard that your eyes water with tears?

Enough Witnesses

Most of us have received spiritual witnesses and felt the impressions of the Holy Spirit many times. More than once, we've said in our hearts, "I really do know there is a God," or "I know the Bible is true," or something to that effect.

Knowing how many times you have felt those tender feelings, from your childhood to today, in quiet little moments or while sitting among large congregations, have you chosen to believe that which you cannot prove for certainty?

At some point, God seems to say to us, "You have received enough witnesses. Now make up your mind."

Do it right now, today, where you are sitting. You know it, and you know you know it. So jump in with both feet and believe it one hundred percent, all the way. Commit. Turn the faucet all the way open.

My Yoke Is Easy

Once we put our full and most earnest belief in Jesus Christ above all else, a beautiful thing begins to happen. In a way that's impossible to fully describe, life gets easier. Learning things the hard way happens less. Awful regrets become less frequent. The tragedy of damaged or destroyed relationships is prevented. Jesus said:

> *"Come unto me, all ye that labor and are heavy laden, and I will give you rest.*
>
> *"Take my yoke upon you, and learn of me; for I am meek and lowly in heart: and ye shall find rest unto your souls.*
>
> *"For my yoke is easy, and my burden is light." (Matthew 11:28-30)*

Many have wondered at this saying. "Really? My yoke is easy? I think it's hard to change my life. I think it's hard to live differently than my friends. Really hard things keep happening to me as I try to fully commit to living the gospel of Jesus Christ."

But hard compared to what? Living without God is what's hard because it's *dark*. When we walk in the dark, we stumble, fall, break things, and never really get anywhere. We struggle with varied addictions. We can't seem to solidly and permanently improve our relationships with others. We squander precious time in our lives chasing what the world says is important, only to later see our wasted potential and the shallowness of it all. We wallow in time wasting or physically harmful habits because they're easy and they allow us to "hide." We needlessly fear things like death, sickness, or even our own weaknesses. The list could go on and on. Eventually we're face to face with sad and even tragic consequences. That's living the hard way.

And living *halfway* in the dark isn't much easier. Many of us don't find life easy because we haven't turned on the light. We haven't had the true gospel experience yet. So we're doubly miserable because we read and hear that life is supposed to be all happy and good, but we're not experiencing it.

But persistently living in the light and power of Christ remedies all of these things. In a deeply satisfying and in a beautiful way, life becomes much, much easier.

> *And we know that all things work together for good*
> *to them that love God (Romans 8:28).*

Everything comes together in ways that we never could have imagined when we believe in, love, and put Christ first.

It works. I testify to you. It all works.

What If I'm Still Not Happy?

Gospel happiness is different from what many people expect. Gospel happiness comes in the form of peace to be content in our circumstances. It is the deep joy of knowing that we have a purpose in life and that we are on the path to fulfilling that purpose. It is the joy of making a difference in someone's life. It is the joy of knowing that God will get you through, come what may.

Joy is much more powerful than laughter and good times. It's not the kind of, "My life is perfect and smooth sailing!" feeling that we often expect. Rick Warren's perspective is deeply insightful:

> *Life is a series of problems: Either you are in one now, you're just coming out of one, or you're getting ready to go into another one. The reason for this is that God is more interested in your **character** than your **comfort**. God is more interested in making your life **holy** than He is in making your life **happy**. We can be reasonably happy here on earth, but that's not the goal of life. The goal is to grow in character, in Christlikeness.*[66]

Here are some common problems in the Twitter era that can cause unhappiness and confusion—even while trying to sincerely love and follow Jesus:

- Emotional, sexual, and physical abuse create deep scars that can remain for years, leaving the victim in a maze of mixed feelings and thoughts. Seek competent professional help. It makes a huge difference.
- Mental and emotional health issues can wreak havoc on our ability to enjoy life. They can even distort our spiritual sensitivity and cause us to feel unloved or that the Spirit of God has forsaken us. Again, seek professional treatment.
- Post-traumatic stress disorder (PTSD) is similar to both of the above. Whether you are a military veteran with actual combat experience or a survivor of abuse or other trauma, know that your ability to feel positive emotions has been affected by PTSD. Seek professional help.
- Sometimes we must face the consequences of prior life choices that take considerable time to unwind. Addictions to foods, drugs, sex, and gambling can leave physical scars or devastating life situations that just aren't easy to cope with or overcome. It's hard to feel blissful when recovering from two hundred pounds of addiction-driven weight gain, serving a jail sentence for sex crimes, or recovering from a recent divorce because of a rabid gambling problem. However, this is where the long-term, eternal perspective of Christ's gospel helps us bear it. Faithfully taking His yoke upon

you is easier than bearing your trials alone or being held in the grips of Satan, only to spiral further down. The Savior's joy—which is different than pleasure or bliss—is real.

- We may need to round out our lives with things that are uplifting and enriching—but not just in the Bible. Jesus and the apostles taught the essential spiritual truths, principles, and commandments required for salvation. Just because they don't teach that we should do yoga specifically, for example, doesn't mean that yoga is not beneficial. Meditation and yoga may be the very thing you need to help you feel dramatically better than you do today. It is erroneous to think that if Jesus didn't say it, it must not be appropriate or beneficial.
- We should benefit from good and wise insights from our fellow men, which we can discern to be useful and appropriate through prayer and prudent judgment. Failing to take care of our bodies, enjoy recreation, and develop our minds—despite sincere discipleship—can still lead to the feeling that we are missing something. And we may be. God desires us to have a complete and well-rounded mortal experience to the degree that our time, means, and circumstances allow.

Your Best Friend Forever

I invite you to "put on your faith glasses" and "drink the living water" by making Jesus your Best Friend Forever (BFF).

- **Believe** in Jesus with the intention to trust and obey him.
- **Favor** Jesus above all others by admiring His wisdom and worshipping Him as the God of the universe.
- **Follow** Jesus by remembering what He did and walking right behind Him.

I promise that as you do, His face will become clearer to you, you will feel His presence more often, and He will guide your thoughts so that you know how to follow Him—even in these modern times.

Love from Above

"Help me overcome my unbelief!"

—Mark 9:24, NIV

My Upward Climb

Can I envision God as a kindly parent standing over his toddler child, watching him try to walk for the first time?

If I hesitate to believe that God is there because of unanswered questions, wouldn't a kindly parent respect my sincerity and stand by, ready to hold me up when I try?

Chapter 23

What If Believing Is Hard for Me?

Many of my believing, actively churchgoing friends who read this chapter said to me, "You should have put that chapter first. That helped me a lot. People might not read it at the end." I suppose they liked it because even those who believe in Christ sometimes sense they can do it better.

However, those who aren't quite ready to believe in Christ find the act of believing to be unnerving or even outright irresponsible. I can fully relate to both points of view, having felt both at different times in my life.

This chapter is offered as a final perspective as to why and how to believe and to help you have the courage to eradicate doubt.

Believing in the Unseen

Whatever your situation, every person reading this—in fact, every person on earth this very moment—believes in things they cannot see.

It's true. You may have never thought of it this way, but there are very few things you really *know* to be true. You have chosen to believe things based on evidence—good evidence, usually. You use your senses, your mind, and your good judgment to decide whether to believe something or not.

For example, you don't know for sure that your teachers, friends, or bosses really know what they're talking about. You listen and either immediately believe it (or not) or you choose to think about it for a while. You may look for more evidence and then decide to believe it or not.

Is Russia for Real?

You don't actually know that the country, Russia, exists unless you've crossed the Russian border, held Russian money in your hand, and heard Russian people speak Russian while standing in Russia. The TV and internet stories you've seen and heard could all be fake. It could all be a big lie. Well, of course, that's outrageous, but think about it. Do you personally, with one hundred percent certainty, know Russia is there? Unless you've been there, you absolutely *do not.*

But you do have a lot of extremely good evidence. So you choose to believe it. What's your evidence? You've seen it on TV, maybe met people from Russia, or have friends who've visited there or watched the Olympics or Googled it. Everyone else seems to believe Russia exists, right? It's all evidence. We can say, "I believe Russia is really there." But relying on our five senses, most of us can't factually say, "I know Russia is really there."

Do You Have Principles?

Here's a different example. You may believe in the Golden Rule: "*Do unto others as you would have them do unto you.*" If you're truly committed to this rule, then you often imagine yourself in another person's situation and are willing to do something for them because you believe it's a good thing to do. People choose to believe in it and live by it.

They believe in and understand something (a principle) they cannot see. Over time, their many positive experiences and feelings inside them become strong evidence that the Golden Rule is truly a good principle. They say with conviction, "I believe in the Golden Rule." But they can't see it and they don't *know* it, but they act a certain way because of it.

Only Five Senses?

We gather evidence in many ways. Most of us have five senses: we can see, hear, smell, taste, and feel. But is that the only way we can gather evidence in deciding what we believe? Obviously not.

With our minds, we reason and listen to people's opinions and stories. We read, we analyze, we look for patterns. We put pieces of evidence together, and we form conclusions. These are all important ways to gather evidence.

We also have something we call our "heart." And we're not talking about that big muscle that pumps blood all day long. We're talking about that deepest part of who we are. We talk about what we are feeling as our "heart." This includes our desires, ambitions, and instincts about what we should do or believe.

This deepest, innermost part of you is your *spirit*. Your spirit is what drives your thinking, desires, and decisions. Regardless of how you were raised or the traits you inherited from your parents, your spirit is the "real you," the part that chooses what you will be. The scriptures tell us that each man and woman has a spirit that came from God (see Job 32:8, Hebrews 12:9). God the Father is the Father of your spirit. He placed each of us into a physical body at the time of our birth.

The fact that you have a spirit is important. If you're not sure whether to believe it or not, just put that idea on up on a shelf and reflect on it now and then. But don't throw it out. When you die, the real you leaves your body and lives on. Your spirit and body separate, like a hand pulled out of a glove.

Philosophy versus Truth

It never will be physically proven that everyone has a spirit that came from God. Your five senses won't help. You can't reason your way into believing it or trying to disprove it either. People who rely on logic and reasoning alone cannot answer that question. Go to Wikipedia and look up "Meaning of Life" (http://en.wikipedia.org/wiki/Meaning_of_life) and the many other articles about philosophy found there. You will see an endless string of peoples' opinions, ideas, and suggestions. They're all different. Throughout the centuries, one theory becomes more popular than another. No philosopher claims to have the facts; each one is just stating his or her own view of things. They're trying to be constructive, and that's a good thing, but it's just an endless debate.

In this book, however, certain things are stated as facts. They are not philosophies, opinions, ideas, or suggestions. *They are founded on revelations from God* and eyewitness accounts of supernatural events. They are based on teachings of the prophets. Prophets are not philosophers. They are not just well-intentioned men with good reasoning. They are handpicked spokesmen for a true, real, and living God who is the Father of us all. You may believe none of that right now, but consider the following story.

Finding the Pearls

On the way home from a nice evening on the town, a woman's genuine pearl necklace breaks and the pearls scatter everywhere—all over the sidewalk and into the street. There's no streetlight, only stars, so it's hard to see anything, let alone recover the pearls. People walking by see the woman and her companion kneeling on the ground and looking for the pearls; some of them stop to help. One person suggests, "I think we should look here," while others say, "No, they must have bounced over there." Some say it's hopeless and keep walking. One man says he doesn't believe there are any pearls because he can't see any and says everyone is wasting their time.

People's opinions and best efforts are not going to find those pearls. It's too dark. What they need is light. Now imagine a thousand floodlights shining directly from above. Problem solved. After some searching, the pearls are recovered.

The meaning of this story?

- The woman and her companion represent each of us as we try to find things that are true but cannot be seen.
- The passersby represent the people around us with their different opinions and good intentions.
- The super-intense light represents the revealed word of God, which makes finding pearls of truth much easier.

Without light, no amount of searching, guessing, or good intentions can solve the problem of finding all those valuable pearls.

The teachings and statements in this book are based on revelations from God. Revelation is like a pure, powerful, bright light from above. It illuminates and lets us see the pure truths God wants us to know.

God is actively involved in trying to teach us, so He sent Jesus and the apostles and our local congregational leaders and ministers. And He communicates with us, spirit to spirit.

Your Spiritual Senses

The fact that we have a spirit makes all the difference in discerning truth. Here's why: our spirit has senses just like our body does. Along with the light of revelation, we can use our spiritual senses to determine what's true and what's false. Here are five keys to get you started on developing your spiritual senses. You'll need *all five* of them to do this:

1. *Don't throw out a spiritual teaching because you don't immediately agree with it.* When a scientist is looking for an answer to a problem, he begins with an idea and gives it some thought. If it doesn't make total sense right away, he may set it aside temporarily, but it's not gone. Every now and then, he thinks about it again, looks at it from a new angle, and tries to see how it might be the answer. It often takes time to connect the dots.

2. *Be willing to believe in things without one hundred percent proof.* Great men of business and science have learned to trust their instincts and believe in things they cannot see—like the future. They had no proof, and neither do we. They believed in what was possible and jumped in with both feet. We don't get all the answers up front. It's not in the plan. Spiritual evidence comes in the form of deep feelings and impressions of the Holy Spirit. This evidence is so real that it borders on proof, but we must still make that choice to believe.
3. *It's okay to change what you believe in.* Coming to know spiritual truth is not a straight-line process. It can involve experimenting. Often the scientist has previously tried a few other things that just haven't worked. Sometimes he hits a wall. We may have believed something was true, but over time, we feel more and more that it just isn't so. So we abandon that belief and search for something that works. If you're afraid to believe in the wrong thing, or make mistakes, good for you. But like the scientist, we learn from our mistakes. We must approach it one step and one decision at a time, understanding that it's a process.
4. *Understand that the mind and heart (spirit) have to work together.* There's a great saying: "What the heart knows today the mind will understand tomorrow." So true. The heart often latches on to an answer before we're able to explain it, even to ourselves. The scientist often experiments because he's had a hunch or a feeling as to what could be true. Don't be afraid to follow your instincts. Begin paying a bit more attention to what your heart tells you. If you rely on your mind alone, you will end up in an infinite loop of questions and more questions. The scientist has to eventually decide which way he's going to go, and that's usually based on a combination of what he's learned through experimentation and a feeling that his next idea is right. The mind can be like a merry-go-round. At some point, you have to get off.
5. *Follow one of the gospel teachings (i.e., commandments) as an experiment, and pay attention to how you feel.* Don't pick one you're already following. Developing your spiritual senses will require that you *do* something, not just think and analyze. Here's

a fun, "scientific" experiment: if you've never tasted chocolate, you'll never know what it's like until you do something about it, until you taste it. If you're not willing to do something different than you do today, you might as well forget it. You'll never know what chocolate tastes like. You'll be forever wondering. So pick one or two things as a test. It's okay to have doubts; if we've never tasted chocolate, it's natural to worry that maybe we won't like it. But maybe we will. It's just an experiment, after all. Give it a few weeks, push yourself through any difficulties, and notice when you feel something positive, good, peaceful, or enlightening—the way a scientist would note that he's starting to get a definitive result. That positive result is one more piece of evidence. Jesus Himself said, "If any man will *do* his will, he shall know of the doctrine, whether it be of God, or whether I speak of myself" (John 7:17, italics added). If you want to know that a teaching (i.e., doctrine) is really from Him, God says we must *do* it. So "taste" it. Do you think the payoffs of honestly seeking this first-hand experience with God and giving belief a try—seeing where it will lead—might benefit you more than just assuming it's not real because you haven't experienced it directly without putting forth effort?

God Understands Our Needs

God does not expect us to blindly believe anything. He completely understands our need for evidence, and because of that, He provides multiple forms of it. But He will never one hundred percent prove anything for us.

You may be thinking, "Why not! If He's really there, why keep us guessing? Seems downright pointless." Well, it turns out there's a very good reason. God wants us to learn certain things while we're here on earth, including certain skills and attributes.

The most basic spiritual skill we must learn in this life is the ability to believe things that are true which we cannot see and then to take action—even when our knowledge of something is not perfect. If God proved everything, we would be unable to learn this essential skill. In other words, we must learn to live by faith. (See Romans 1:17.)

Please keep that idea bouncing around in your mind and ponder it now and then. It explains a lot about why this earth life is the way it is.

Is There a God or Not?

Let's consider evidence for the question, "Does God exist?" First of all, what evidence is there that God does *not* exist? There is actually no evidence whatsoever. None. One may say, "What about the big bang theory—that the universe started from one massive explosion?" I believe in that theory myself, but that doesn't mean God was not involved in some way. It doesn't disprove that God exists. That would be like saying, "I don't believe farmers exist because look at all of the crops that come out of the field all by themselves." Who prepared the soil, planted the seeds, and watched over it all as it grew?

Just like the air, we may not be able to see God, but we may see and feel the effects of His existence. What evidences are there that God *does* exist? A great deal:

- *The order, structure, design, beauty, variety, and harmony of our physical world,* and the multitude of stars we see at night. Seriously, is it more likely that the stars, earth, and your own life all popped into being by chance or that there is some form of higher, organizing intelligence at work in the universe?
- *The writings and teachings of hundreds of prophets over the years*, captured in the scriptures. Many prophets stated that they personally saw God "face to face" along with other heavenly visitors. (For example, see Genesis 32:30 and Exodus 33:11.) Are they all liars? Should we not give some weight to all those testimonies? Many gave their lives defending what they said. (I strongly recommend reading the short but powerful book *More Than a Carpenter*, by Josh McDowell and Sean McDowell. It presents a powerful, well-researched set of arguments that Jesus Christ actually was God and that the apostles' testimonies of the resurrected Christ had to be real. If science and logic are important to you, read this book.)
- *Miracles.* There are dramatic, eye-popping miracles recorded in the scriptures. Many of us have witnessed smaller miracles, things that seemed impossible before they happened. There are countless

stories from people of all faiths throughout the world who have experienced miracles and events that are impossible to explain outside of God's hand.

- *Communication from God directly to your mind and your heart.* This comes from God's Spirit to your spirit. It is more powerful, important, and convincing than any other form of evidence. And you can learn to recognize it.

How Can I Recognize Spiritual Communication?

Communication from God is usually a combination of feelings of peace and clear thoughts—at the same time. You feel that you simply know something is true. You don't know why you suddenly know it, but you do. That's why many people say, "I see the light."

Sometimes you will feel emotional. The insights and feelings of happiness that you feel all at once are often so powerful that you may have tears.

Some people say they feel a warmth within them. It's their heart. Did you ever see the movie *E.T. the Extra-Terrestrial* (1982, Universal Pictures)? At the end of the movie, the little alien's heart glows red when his ship comes near, ready to take him home. That's actually a great analogy of how the Spirit of God works. When God is near and teaching us, it makes us feel at home. Our true self—our spiritual self—resonates with God. It glows, swells, and burns because He is near, and we are briefly connected to Him.

Ask God

Most often, if you want to communicate with God, you have to start the process. Jesus said, "Ask and it will be given to you" (Matthew 7:7, NIV). If "talking" to God seems weird or uncomfortable, a perfectly good way to ask is something like this:

"God, if you are there, I could really use some help right now. I don't understand [such and such]. Will you please help me? Will you help me understand and recognize your answer? If you're there, I'm willing to believe it, but I need some guidance. Please teach me. In Jesus's name, amen."

"Amen" is simply the traditional ending to a prayer, and it means "truly" or "so it is."

Believe on the Name of Jesus

There is great power associated with the name of Jesus. Even for those who don't know much about Him, when we believe on just His name, we are opening a channel of light—a fiber-optic channel of light to the heavens. And the more we know about Him, the brighter this light can become. But it can start with simply the name of Jesus Christ.

Did you ever buy a product where the directions on the label said, "For best results, do such and such"? I'm going to say the same thing: for best results in discovering truth, believe on the name of Jesus. Let your heart feel it, and let your mind say and repeat, "I believe in Jesus Christ" every day. Let that faith grow, and you will find light and understanding flowing in. Don't try to force your learning. Learn at a pace that is right for you, according to God's understanding of who you are and what you need. If that's just too much of a stretch for you right now, I respect that, but please be open to the idea. Just be willing to believe once you begin recognizing the evidence.

Putting It All Together

In summary,

- You already believe and act on many things you can't see and can't prove through your senses.
- Gathering evidence is a natural and important part of learning truth.
- You have a spirit that has the ability to sense right and wrong, truth and error.
- The greatest evidence you can receive will be communication directly to your spirit—a feeling of light, understanding, peace, and confidence—all pretty much at the same time.
- Ask God questions. Keep reading the scriptures, thinking, asking, and waiting.

- As you read and reread the stories of Jesus throughout this book, let them stay a while. Picture the events in your mind. Give your heart some time to connect the teachings and stories to your questions and life experiences. Understanding will come.

My Personal Witness

I want you to know that in addition to all of the evidence and reasoning above, the guy at the keyboard writing these words right now has a witness of the truth of these things. I know by the power of the Holy Spirit that the things I have written are true. I know through the depth of my life experiences that living the gospel of Jesus Christ works. I've received enough witnesses. I have committed one hundred percent. My faucet is wide open, and the water flowing in is intense. I know that Jesus of Nazareth was not just a man. He was the Son of God. He was resurrected and lives today. His teachings help us do what we were sent here to do so that we can be truly happy—in this life and in eternity. I testify that you can know it too.

The real voyage of discovery consists not in seeking new landscapes but in having new eyes.

—Marcel Proust

Notes

All scripture quotations are taken from the King James Version (KJV) of the Holy Bible unless otherwise indicated. Quotation marks have been added to KJV excerpts where people are speaking in order to create a consistent reading experience with the modern Bible translations that are also included in this book.

Introduction

1. Jessica Brown, "Is Social Media Bad for You? The Evidence and the Unknowns," *BBC*, January 5, 2018. http://www.bbc.com/future/story/20180104-is-social-media-bad-for-you-the-evidence-and-the-unknowns. Note: This is a comprehensive and balanced perspective that cites numerous studies. See also: James Emery White, *Meet Generation Z: Understanding and Reaching the New Post-Christian World,* (Ada: Baker Books, 2017), which presents an in-depth analysis of the rising generation and impacts of immersion in social media and instant access to information.
2. Katherine Hobson, "Feeling Lonely? Too Much Time On Social Media May Be Why." *NPR*, March 6, 2017. https://www.npr.org/sections/health-shots/2017/03/06/518362255/feeling-lonely-too-much-time-on-social-media-may-be-why. See also: Nick Zagorski, "Using Many Social Media Platforms Linked With Depression, Anxiety Risk," *Psychiatric News*, January 17, 2017. https://psychnews.psychiatryonline.org/doi/full/10.1176/appi.pn.2017.1b16. See also: Jane Wakefield, "Is social media causing childhood depression?" *BBC*, February 10, 2018. https://www.bbc.com/news/technology-4270588

Chapter 1: Before Christ

3. Deuteronomy 30:1–20
4. Acts 10:43
5. Cunningham Geike, *The Life and Words of Christ.* (New York: American Book Exchange, 1880, 57)
6. Eric M. Meyers and James F. Strange, *Archaeology, the Rabbis, & Early Christianity.* (Nashville: Abingdon, 1981) Note: Although Geike cites Jewish historian Josephus's assertion that there were many towns in Galilee, the smallest of which had a population above fifteen thousand, modern archaeologists believe Nazareth had a population under 500 inhabitants.

7. New Testament Seminary Teacher Manual, Lesson 6: Matthew 1-2. https://www.lds.org/manual/new-testament-seminary-teacher-manual/matthew/lesson-6-matthew-1-2?lang=eng See also, Steve Rudd, "The Three Stage Ritual of Bible Marriages," *The Interactive Bible.* http://www.bible.ca/marriage/ancient-jewish-three-stage-weddings-and-marriage-customs-ceremony-in-the-bible.htm

Chapter 2: The Lamb of God

8. Albert Barnes, *Barnes' Notes on the New Testament*, (Grand Rapids, Michigan: Kregel Publications, 1962). http://biblehub.com/commentaries/luke/2-7.htm
9. James E. Talmage, *Jesus the Christ: A Study of the Messiah and His Mission According to Holy Scriptures both Ancient and Modern,* (Salt Lake City: Deseret Book Company, 1982, 106)
10. Randy Alcorn, *Shepherd Status* in *Come, Thou Long-Expected Jesus*, ed. Nancy Guthrie (Wheaton, IL: Crossway Books, 2008, 85–89)
11. Talmage, 35–36
12. "What does the Bible teach about the Trinity?" *GotQuestions.org.* https://www.gotquestions.org/Trinity-Bible.html

Chapter 3: Wild Man Preaching

13. Justin Taylor, "7 Differences Between Galilee and Judea in the Time of Jesus," *The Gospel Coalition.* Accessed June 9, 2018. https://www.thegospelcoalition.org/blogs/justin-taylor/7-differences-between-galilee-and-judea-in-the-time-of-jesus/. See also Peter J. Leithart, "No. 22: Galilee of the Gentiles," *BiblicalHorizons.com.* http://www.biblicalhorizons.com/biblical-horizons/no-22-galilee-of-the-gentiles/
14. D. Kelly Ogden, *Where Jesus Walked: The Land and Culture of New Testament Times,* (Salt Lake City: Deseret Book Company, 1991, 27). See also: Nazareth Village, "First Century Travel." Accessed January 7, 2018. http://www.nazarethvillage.com/discover/findings-research/first-century-travel/

Chapter 4: Temptations

15. Talmage, 166
16. Ogden, 11
17. Frederic W. Farrar, *The Life of Christ*, (New York: E. P. Dutton & Company, 1893, 88).

Chapter 5: The Beginning of Miracles

18. *The Holy Bible*, Preface to the English Standard Version (Wheaton: Crossway, 2011).
19. BibleHub.com, citing *Ellicott's Commentary for English Readers* notes for John 2:6. http://biblehub.com/commentaries/john/2-6.htm
20. Talmage, 146

21. John MacArthur, *The Gospel According to Jesus: What is Authentic Faith?* Revised, Anniversary, Expanded Edition, (Grand Rapids: Zondervan, 2009), Kindle, 8th paragraph under The Reality of Redemption.

Chapter 6: My Father's House

22. Geike, 346
23. Geike, 346
24. Talmage, 155
25. Talmage, 156

Chapter 7: The Woman of Samaria

26. Farrar, 148

Chapter 8: Rejected By His Own

27. Chad Spigel, "First Century Synagogues," *Bible Odyssey*. https://www.bibleodyssey.org:443/en/places/related-articles/first-century-synagogues
28. Tim Hegg, "The Public Reading of the Scriptures in the 1st Century Synagogue," *TorahResource.com*. https://www.torahresource.com/EnglishArticles/TriennialCycle.pdf
29. Talmage, 180
30. Note: Some have suggested that the angry mob seeking to throw Jesus over the cliff *included* His family members. We know that some of Jesus's brothers did not believe in Him. (See John 7:5.) It is not inconceivable that they felt justified in participating in the violence since—in their view—Jesus was making an outrageously false claim in the synagogue that day. http://www1.cbn.com/BibleArcheology/archive/2010/12/19/five-things-you-didnt-know-about-nazareth
31. With some empathy for the Jews of Jesus's day, we should note that several false Messiahs had presented themselves as the deliverers of Israel and had failed miserably. (See Geike, pp. 99–100.) The Jewish people at that time were beyond eager for the arrival of their Messiah, but they had good reason to be cautious and alert to deception.

Chapter 9: Healing and Forgiveness

32. Farrar, 415
33. Talmage, 188–189
34. Sidney Lee (ed.), *The Autobiography of Edward, Lord Herbert of Cherbury*, revised edition (London: Routledge, 1906)

Chapter 10: What Matters Most?

35. Robb Ladd, "Climbing the Ladder of Success ... Successfully," *FamilyLife*. https://www.familylife.com/articles/topics/life-issues/challenges/workaholism/climbing-the-ladder-of-success-successfully/

36. John J. Parsons, "The Beatitudes of Jesus, Recited in Hebrew," *Hebrew for Christians*. http://www.hebrew4christians.com/Scripture/Brit_Chadashah/Beatitudes/beatitudes.html
37. Ibid.

Chapter 11: What's in It for Me?

38. David A. Bednar, "We Believe in Being Chaste," *Ensign*, May 2013. https://www.lds.org/general-conference/2013/04/we-believe-in-being-chaste?lang=eng
39. Random Acts of Kindness (RAK) is a website and worldwide movement. Their vision: "We believe that the world will be a significantly better place if we encourage the spread of kindness in schools, communities and homes—so we try to enable that in whatever way we can." Visit them online: https://www.randomactsofkindness.org/kindness-ideas
40. Martin Luther King, *A Knock at Midnight: Inspiration from the Great Sermons of the Reverend Martin Luther King, Jr.*, (New York: Warner Books, 2000)
41. David A. Bednar, "The Character of Christ," Brigham Young University–Idaho religion symposium, Jan. 25, 2003
42. Dennis R. Bratcher, "The English Term Perfect: Biblical and Philosophical Tensions." *The Voice: Biblical and Theological Resources for Growing Christians*. http://www.crivoice.org/perfect.html
43. Ben, "So You Believe the Bible But Still Struggle With Pornography. Now What?" *PlainSimpleFaith.com*. http://www.plainsimplefaith.com/2013/06/struggle-with-pornography/. Note: The "Spiritual Warfare" section in this website is full of outstanding, practical advice.
44. Margaret Willden Willes, "Shyness and Introversion: Looking In, Turning Out," *Ensign*, July, 2017. https://www.lds.org/ensign/2017/07/young-adults/shyness-and-introversion-looking-in-turning-out?lang=eng

Chapter 13: Save Me!

45. Talmage, 284

Chapter 14: The Fish, Coin, and the King

46. Talmage, 396
47. Talmage, 384
48. Talmage, 383–386

Chapter 15: Help of the Helpless

49. Talmage, 332
50. Henry F. Lyte, "Abide With Me," *Hymntime.com*. http://www.hymntime.com/tch/htm/a/b/i/abidewme.htm

Chapter 16: The Bread of Life

51. Talmage, 342

Chapter 17: Last Trip to Jerusalem

52. Joseph S. Exell and Henry Donald Maurice Spence-Jones (ed.), *Pulpit Commentary* on BibleHub.com. http://biblehub.com/luke/9-45.htm
53. Flavius Josephus, *The Wars of the Jews, Book VII* (AD 75, translated by William Whiston, 1737). http://www.sacred-texts.com/jud/josephus/war-7.htm
54. Biblical Archeology Society Staff, "A Tomb in Jerusalem Reveals the History of Crucifixion and Roman Crucifixion Methods," *Bible History Daily* (2011). https://www.biblicalarchaeology.org/daily/biblical-topics/crucifixion/a-tomb-in-jerusalem-reveals-the-history-of-crucifixion-and-roman-crucifixion-methods/

Chapter 18: The Atonement

55. Dieter F. Uchtdorf, "Lord, Is It I?" *Ensign*, October 2014. https://www.lds.org/general-conference/2014/10/lord-is-it-i?lang=eng
56. "Onward Christian Soldiers," Original lyrics by Sabine Baring-Gould in 1865 and music by Arthur S. Sullivan in 1871
57. Lehman Strauss, "The Atonement of Christ," *Bible.org*. https://bible.org/article/atonement-christ

Chapter 19: I Have Overcome the World

58. This is a fascinating article that analyzes the pressures on Pilate as well as the mentality of the crowds on the decisive day of the crucifixion: J. W. Welch, "The Factor of Fear in the Trial of Jesus," *Jesus Christ: Son of God, Savior,* ed. Paul H. Peterson, Gary L. Hatch, and Laura D. Card (Provo, UT: Religious Studies Center, Brigham Young University, 2002), 284–312. https://rsc.byu.edu/archived/jesus-christ-son-god-savior/13-factor-fear-trial-jesus
59. Biblical Archeology Society Staff, "A Tomb in Jerusalem Reveals the History of Crucifixion and Roman Crucifixion Methods," *Bible History Daily* (2011). https://www.biblicalarchaeology.org/daily/biblical-topics/crucifixion/a-tomb-in-jerusalem-reveals-the-history-of-crucifixion-and-roman-crucifixion-methods/
60. There are many excellent addiction recovery resources online. Simply search for "addiction recovery for Christians."

Chapter 20: It Is Finished

61. A. G. Shlomo, *Matthew: A Rabbinic Source Commentary and Language Study Bible* (Sefer Press, 2015, 592). This work cites Misn. Shekalim, c. 8. sect. 5. Shernot Rabba, sect. 50. fol. 144. 2. Bernidbar Rabba, sect. 4. fol. 183. 2. as the source.

Chapter 21: From Death to Life

62. Albert Mohler, "Do Christians Still Believe in the Resurrection of the Body?" *AlbertMohler.com*, April 7, 2006. https://albertmohler.com/2006/04/07/do-christians-still-believe-in-the-resurrection-of-the-body/
63. Catholic Answers, "Resurrection of the Body." https://www.catholic.com/tract/resurrection-of-the-body

Chapter 22: The Eye of Faith

64. See 1 John 3:23 and Matthew 4:19.
65. Dieter F. Uchtdorf, "Be Not Afraid, Only Believe," *Ensign*, November 2015. https://www.lds.org/general-conference/2015/10/be-not-afraid-only-believe?lang=eng
66. Rick Warren, "An Interview by Paul Bradshaw with Rick Warren," SalemChristianHomeSchool.com. https://www.salemchristianhomeschool.com/478/custom/14359. See also PastorRick.com, "God's Purpose in Suffering," http://pastorrick.com/devotional/english/god's-purpose-in-suffering.

About the Author

R. Christian Bohlen grew up as a first-generation American, the son of immigrants from the Amsterdam region of the Netherlands, where Dutch was spoken continually in their small-town Pennsylvania home. Their food, customs, and European way of thinking were all very different from American culture. As a boy, Christian felt conspicuously different and disoriented. His parents were deeply religious, quiet, studious classical musicians living in a community where shotguns, deer hunting, American football, and four-wheel drive trucks were the norm.

Unsettled by the contrasts in his life, including the confusion of the hippie 1960s, the rock 'n' roll, drug culture of the 1970s, the influence of atheist friends, and serious mental health issues of family and friends, Christian's anxiety to make sense of his surroundings aroused a life-long determination to grasp the world around him and make it understandable for others—especially the things of eternity.

By the sum of his life experiences, God forged the heart of a teacher in him.

He earned a BS in applied mathematics with a minor in education and an MS in communications (instructional design and organizational learning) from Clarion University of Pennsylvania. He has enjoyed careers in both private education and corporate training, resulting in prestigious personal and team awards including the Brandon Hall Silver (2013) and ISPI Outstanding Human Performance Intervention (2015) team awards. He holds a Project Management Professional (PMP) certification and typically functions as both a program manager and lead instructional designer.

He has been active in church in Pennsylvania and Virginia for many years, serving as a youth and adult Sunday School teacher and ministry leader. He speaks regularly at multiple congregations and oversees a prison ministry program serving the central Pennsylvania region. He is an active member of Lions International, the largest service organization in the world, and recently served as president of his local Lions club. He and his wife are also certified Laughter Yoga leaders. (Find Laughter Yoga near you! It's too funny!)

Christian once recalled, "My years working at a drug and alcohol rehab for juveniles were a life-changing experience. One incident stands out. A certain young man was unusually angry one day. When I approached him about it, he agonized, 'My counselor gave me a Bible. I can't *understand* it!' He had trouble reading, and I knew he didn't have a chance of understanding even the 'easy' modern versions of the Bible. I wanted to give him something simple to help him find Christ, like a tour through the life of Jesus with me at his side explaining what it all meant, while making sure he witnessed the majesty of Jesus Christ for himself by the power of the Holy Spirit. But I couldn't find anything like that. So, that's where the initial concept for this book came from."

Christian continued writing and seeking God's guidance for over twenty years, applying his professional skills as an instructional designer to carefully align the structure and style of his writings to the needs of modern, busy, or skeptical readers who may not be familiar with the Bible or Christianity.

Learn more and subscribe at http://hislifeandmine.com and @hislifeandmine on Facebook and Twitter.